Mel

Hap

Wishing you all
the best on your
future discovery

'We spend so much of our lives at work. In a changing world, understanding how to make work "work better" for people is essential. *LoveWork* is a simple guide to help.'

'Let your dream, vision and deep sense of purpose be your guide to life and work. *LoveWork* will show you how to recognize and articulate your vision.'

'Reading *LoveWork* is an investment in you and your career. It helps you understand the "why" in your work and increase the impact of your efforts. There are no false promises of waving magic wands and working happily ever after. Instead it enables you to discover what time well spent looks like for you and shares practical tools and insightful stories to help you achieve it.'

'I am a great believer in the part that serendipity plays to shape our futures. Read *LoveWork* to accelerate your evolution.'

'Work provides an important opportunity to leave things in a better place and ready for the next generation. *LoveWork* will inspire you to do this and more.'

'Focus on creating a great place to work where everyone can be their true selves and reach their potential. This is at the heart of *LoveWork*.'

'*LoveWork* resonates with the essence of who we are at The Standard in offering experiences to our guests that enrich their lives while simultaneously offering experiences to our teams that open up worlds of possibilities for them. The two go hand in hand. Like *LoveWork* can and should.'

'As a father I have noticed that the next generation are determined to live different lives and make different trade-offs. Young people want to work hard, whilst prioritizing work that they enjoy. They will not tolerate what the previous generation did. Work should be fulfilling and *LoveWork* helps you make changes for a better future.'

Errol Williams, Vice President, WeWork

'We are living and working longer and it's important that we use this time well. I have found that being with like-minded people who are motivated by a common purpose really matters. It also helps to have fun along the way! *LoveWork* advocates both.'

Sam Barrell, Chief Operating Officer, The Francis Crick Institute

'Let's face it: we spend 20-25% of our adult waking hours at work, so life is too short to not *LoveWork*. As *The Spare Room* was designed to help you define your social legacy, this book enables you to *LoveWork* and live in a more purposeful way.'

Emily Chang, Chief Executive Officer, China, McCann
Worldgroup and author of The Spare Room

'If you dread Mondays, if work is a chore, YOU MUST READ THIS BOOK. It doesn't have to be like that. Indeed, it shouldn't. The case studies alone are incredibly helpful... so many stories of people who have turned it around – and you can too. And if you're a business leader, use *LoveWork* to create an organisation where people are happy and fulfilled.'

Greg Jackson, Chief Executive Officer, Octopus Energy

Love Work

LoveWork

The Seven Steps to Thrive at Work

BEN RENSHAW AND SOPHIE DEVONSHIRE

JOHN
MURRAY
LEARNING

First published in Great Britain by John Murray Learning in 2021
An imprint of John Murray Press
A division of Hodder & Stoughton Ltd,
An Hachette UK company

1

A CIP catalogue record for this title is available from the British Library

Hardback ISBN 978 1 529 36853 6
eBook ISBN 978 1 529 36855 0

Typeset by KnowledgeWorks Global Ltd.

Printed and bound in Great Britain by Clays Ltd, Elcograf S.p.A.

John Murray Press policy is to use papers that are natural, renewable and recyclable products and made from wood grown in sustainable forests. The logging and manufacturing processes are expected to conform to the environmental regulations of the country of origin.

John Murray Press
Carmelite House
50 Victoria Embankment
London EC4Y 0DZ

www.johnmurraypress.co.uk

For our children, India, Ziggy and Zebedee and Rosie
and Gigi. Thank you for inspiring us.

May you (and the next generation of those who will
enter the world of work) learn to find what you will
love and learn how to love what you do.

Contributors

The following people gave their insight and time with incredible generosity, providing in-depth interviews or insightful quotes. They will be referenced by name and role in the book:

Amar Lalvani, Chief Executive Officer, Standard International

Amy C. Edmondson, Novartis Professor of Leadership and Management, Harvard Business School and author of *The Fearless Organization*

Andreas Thrasy, Chairman, New World Hospitality

Angela Brav, President, Hertz International

Barry Robinson, President and Managing Director International Operations at Wyndham Vacation Clubs, Wyndham Destinations

Brian Woodhead, Customer Service Director, Transport for London

David Woodward, former Executive Vice President, President and Chief Executive Officer at Heinz Europe, Founder and Chief Executive Officer of Woodward Leadership LTD

Emily Chang, Chief Executive Officer, China, McCann Worldgroup

Emma Gilthorpe, Chief Operating Officer, Heathrow

Errol Williams, Vice President, WeWork

Graham Alexander, Founder, The Alexander Partnership

Henry Braithwaite, Founder, Lead Forensics

Joel Burrows, Chief Executive Officer, Ghirardelli

Jamie Bunce, Chief Executive Officer, Inspired Villages

John Holland-Kaye, Chief Executive Officer, Heathrow

Jonathan Coen, Security Director, Heathrow

Jonathan Mills, Chief Executive Officer, EMEA, Choice Hotels

Khaled Ismail, Vice President Communications, Europe, Central Asia, Middle East and Africa, Tetra Pak

Keith Barr, Chief Executive Officer, InterContinental Hotels Group

Dr Kai Reinhardt, Professor of Digital Management, Organization and HR, University of Technology and Economics Berlin

Laura Miller, Executive Vice President, Chief Information Officer, Macy's

Nick Dent, Director of Customer Operations, London Underground

Oliver Bonke, Chief Executive Officer, Middle East, Europe, India, Americas, Shangri-La Hotels and Resorts

Paul Snyder, Executive Vice President Stewardship, Tillamook County Creamery Association

Paula Stannett, Chief People Officer, Heathrow

Renée Elliott, Founder, Planet Organic and Co-Founder, Beluga Bean

Richard Boyatzis, Distinguished University Professor, Case Western Reserve University, co-author of *Primal Leadership* and *Helping People Change*

Richard Solomons, Chairman, Rentokil Initial

Sam Barrell, Chief Operating Officer, The Francis Crick Institute

Siân Evans, Director of Leadership and Colleague Experience, Simplyhealth

Sian Keane, Chief People Officer, Farfetch

Staynton Brown, Director Diversity & Inclusion and Talent, Transport for London

Stephen McCall, Chief Executive Officer, edyn

Wim Dejonghe, Senior Partner, Allen & Overy LLP

Contents

Foreword

I discovered the work I love to do by mistake. In the mid-1990s I had the good fortune to join an interdisciplinary team of researchers undertaking a ground-breaking study of medication errors in hospitals. As part of the study, trained nurse investigators painstakingly gathered data about these potentially devastating human errors over a six-month period, hoping to shed light on their actual incidence in hospitals. Meanwhile, I observed how caregivers in hospital units worked, trying to understand the structures and cultures under which they laboured in this lifesaving work, and seeking to gain insight into the conditions under which errors might happen in these busy, customized, occasionally chaotic operations. Here, teamwork and coordination could be a matter of life or death. I also distributed a survey to assess systematically how well the different patient care units worked as teams.

Along the way, I accidentally stumbled into the importance of psychological safety, which is broadly defined as a climate in which people are comfortable expressing and being themselves, despite the interpersonal risks they take when doing so. More specifically, when people have psychological safety at work, they feel comfortable asking for help and sharing concerns or mistakes without fear of embarrassment or retribution. They are confident that they can speak up and won't be humiliated, ignored or blamed. They know they can ask questions when they are unsure about something. They tend to trust and respect their colleagues. When a work environment has reasonably high psychological safety, good things happen: mistakes are reported quickly so that prompt corrective action can be taken; seamless coordination across groups or departments is enabled, and potentially game-changing ideas for innovation are shared.

My accidental discovery of this interpersonal climate factor occurred when the survey data suggested that better teamwork (itself enabled by more highly rated team leaders) was correlated with higher (not lower!) error rates. This surprising result started me thinking. Perhaps, I wondered, better teams don't make more mistakes, but rather are more willing and able to speak up about them. This meant that we didn't have the complete picture, and more research was needed to show that this was in fact true. In short, psychological safety is a crucial source for individuals, teams and organizations to do their best work.

The purpose of *LoveWork* is to give you a proven methodology for discovering or recovering the work you love. The seven formative ideas act as a roadmap for navigating the big questions associated with work including:

- Why work?
- What is your work about?
- How can you do your best work?

Early work experiences are pivotal; they shape our work expectations – for better or for worse. On a personal note, I was fortunate that my first job after college was to work as an engineer with Buckminster Fuller. An inventor and educator, Buckminster Fuller was renowned for his comprehensive perspective on the most crucial challenges faced by society, such as inadequate housing and food, or climate change, and advocated design science as a way of exercising systems thinking to do 'more with less'. Working with him gave me the opportunity to be immersed in meaningful projects with a curious and respectful person. Following my work with Buckminster Fuller, going into an ordinary workplace would have been challenging, and I was fortunate to continue to find work throughout my career that allowed me to express myself and contribute to meaningful enterprises in respectful, learning-oriented communities. I credit Buckminster Fuller with showing me how work can be fuelled by a relentless curiosity and commitment to helping make the world a better place. My own career journey later took me to Harvard for a PhD in Organizational Behaviour, which ultimately allowed me to become the Novartis Professor of Leadership and Management at

Harvard Business School, a chair established to support the study of human interactions that lead to the creation of successful enterprises that contribute to the betterment of society.

My research examines psychological safety and cross-boundary teaming within and between organizations. I am particularly interested in how leaders enable the learning and collaboration that are so vital to performance in a dynamic environment. In one stream of my research, I study collaboration among diverse experts to solve challenging problems in cities. In this domain, teaming across industry boundaries is increasingly important. Yet, teaming and learning among diverse experts, facing high uncertainty, requires facing both interpersonal and technical risks, and leadership is a powerful force in helping people face and overcome those risks. A second stream of my research examines how leaders create psychological safety in support of organizational agility, as needed to thrive in fast-paced, challenging, uncertain contexts.

I believe that there is a strong link between the creation of psychological safety and *LoveWork*. I am writing this foreword in the midst of COVID-19, and this situation has brought home in a particularly dramatic way how everyone needs to be clear and transparent about what we are up against – specifically, the enormous uncertainty, complexity and challenges that we face. I call this 'setting the stage', and in this case it requires people to be clear about what they need to do their best work and inviting them to speak up about it.

What are you seeing? What concerns do you have? What questions do you need to ask? What actions do you need to take? Responses from yourself and others need to be given in a forward-looking and appreciative way. We are all vulnerable in the face of unprecedented challenges. When we name them and ask for help it opens the door for new possibilities to emerge.

Another key factor for *LoveWork* is the motivation to do great work. To be driven in the pursuit of excellence means adopting a learning and growth mindset where you are willing to stretch yourself to get smarter and better. The combination of focusing on mastery and challenging yourself to improve unleashes your ideas and helps you to make progress towards things that may have been previously cited as impossible.

In *LoveWork* the authors expand these concepts and offer a step-by-step framework for doing the work you love and loving the work you do. It is filled with illustrative scenario-based examples to nurture the free expression of ideas and help you thrive. In my book *The Fearless Organization* I state: 'The fearless organization is something to continually strive toward rather than to achieve once and for all. It's a never-ending and dynamic journey.' My belief is that your quest to discover or recover the work you love and your willingness to speak up, ask questions, debate vigorously and continue to learn will result in great things happening. It's not that it's easy, or always enjoyable, but investing the effort and living with the challenges pays off. I hope this book will help you do just that.

Amy C. Edmondson,
Novartis Professor of Leadership and
Management, Harvard Business School

Introduction

What does good look like?
What does great feel like?

A staggering 90,000 hours of our lives (on average) will be spent working. Around 20 to 25 per cent of our waking adult life. A quarter of our allotted hours.

This means our relationship with work is therefore one of the most critical parts of our life. It can be a challenging relationship; frustrating, and far from straightforward. Or it can be rewarding, satisfying and incredibly fulfilling. Sometimes our relationship with work can be all these things at the same time.

This is, of course, also a relationship which will continuously evolve. Across our lives we change as people which will inevitably change how we work. The world of work is also developing at an accelerated rate. Right now, we are all moving into a new and more dynamic world. More options are becoming possible and changes are happening fast.

Take this opportunity to pause, reflect and review your work and your plans for the future. It's a good moment in time to ask some key questions, to analyse your thoughts and feelings about work: How will you know that you are doing the work you love? What does good look like? What does great feel like? And do you believe it is possible to discover (or recover) a better relationship with work?

These questions are for each and every one of us. Questions to firmly ask ourselves when we are at a stage in our lives when we need to make important decisions about our future, or at any moment when we can take time to think about what we want. At the heart of these questions and at the core of this book is the insight that we always have agency, we always have choice, and – whatever our circumstances – we always have the option to effectively shape our work.

The reality, however, is that we often forget our own agency. We focus on the responsibility of the other – our employer perhaps, our partners, our workplace. And frequently we all find ourselves operating on autopilot. We can sleepwalk (or 'sleep-work') through thousands of hours until an externally driven event jolts us into reconsidering how we should navigate our work choices. Sometimes this is a role change or redundancy, other times a personal tragedy or life-change. In certain situations it is only when your relationship with work breaks down and you face 'irreconcilable differences' that reassessment and re-evaluations take place.

This book is designed to help you consciously choose and drive what happens, to consider what role you can play in sculpting a positive work relationship from here on in. Reading this is designed to stimulate your thinking around how to make those precious 90,000 hours as rewarding for you as possible, to help you love what you do. We believe it is possible to find, rediscover or nurture your love of your work, and we have outlined a journey of seven tangible steps to help you get there.

What should you expect from this book? Please, don't go further if you are wanting a careers guidance manual or a preaching, teaching 'how to be successful' diatribe. This is *your* one life, and everyone's work dreams and dislikes are complex and as unique to them as a fingerprint or the stripes of a zebra. Do read on if you're interested in feasting on a smorgasbord of stimulation, stories, tools and techniques to help you develop a game plan for a working life that works brilliantly for you.

Think of this as supportive, challenging guidance for one of the most significant relationships in your life. Like any relationship, your relationship with work will benefit enormously from care, questioning, nurturing and attention. We're here to help make that easier.

We're here to support you by sharing simple steps which will help you discover how to do more of what you love and love more of what you do. And along the way, to share ideas and perspectives from others who have spent time working out how to make work better (or brilliant) for them. We have found that one of the quickest short-cuts to success in work generally is often to learn from others (their mistakes or their experience), so sharing some work life examples from a diverse range of people, we believe, will accelerate your new LoveWork plan.

For clarity, though, please don't think of this as a 'survival guide'. We want you to aim higher than surviving at work. We want to help you thrive, to help you flourish, to help you feel good about being at work (wherever that physically is).

Our title is, in part, a provocation. Not everyone can or will love their work all the time. Work is normally less fulfilling as a relationship for most people than their human relationships. But following our research and conversations with others we have seen that it is possible to love what you do more often, to rekindle a love that has faltered or to discover a new love for your work. Let's make work work better for you, for your business and for your precious life.

Like all relationships, your ability to feel good about your work is linked to other people. We would encourage you to be confident about sharing the 'love' word at work. One of our contributors Paul Snyder captures this perspective in his words.

> Love is the most underused word in business. It seems to be incongruous that as human beings we carve out 8–10 hours of our day to live in environments where love is supposed to be absent! I believe that most people love some of what they do, but what's really important is to love who they work with. Can anyone say 'I love my job!' without loving who they work with? Love has been programmed out of business and we need to bring it back. Be open to loving the people you work with and letting them know as it would be very difficult to develop a mindset of loving your work if you can't share it.

There is the potential of much positivity for you promised in these pages, but we are devoutly practical and realistic about this. Happily ever after is an overclaim for any relationship. We know that you can't feel honeymoon-happy every moment of your 90,000 hours, any more than a love affair can't be all romps and roses. However, we've discovered seven steps which can help make your relationship with your work more meaningful. These will help you stop counting the hours at work and instead make those hours count.

Importantly, we want to recognize that the idea of 'work–life' balance feels dangerous in some ways. While rest and time not working is always a necessity, the idea that work is perceived to be the opposite of life is far from ideal. For those of us lucky enough to have employment which can offer mastery, purpose, connections and interest, to dismiss a quarter of our waking hours as 'not living' feels wrong. Should all our focus be on allowing or finding ways to 'have more life?' Instead, could we explore how we can make work more meaningful and rewarding; to bring life to our work?

> 'People talk about work–life balance. But the idea of balancing one against
> another makes no sense. My work isn't against my life – work is my life.'

A Noel Coward quote which Stephen Fry keeps above his desk

About us: our stories and what drove us to write this book

Like everyone, our personal history shapes where we are with work today (and what we want to do in the future). This book is written by two very different people, with different backgrounds but a shared interest in uncovering true work love for others. Ben's personal story began inside the world-renowned Yehudi Menuhin School, a prestigious hothouse nestled in the beautiful Surrey countryside, where he trained as a classical violinist. The school gave him early exposure to those who saw their work as a calling. Ben has a clear memory of observing the founder of the school, the visionary Lord Menuhin – then in the later stages of his life and struggling with his health – as he placed a violin under his chin and was transported to a dimension of complete flow. While he played, Lord Menuhin would become fully energized and present, and the magic of his playing would touch everyone fortunate enough to be there. Despite Ben's great talent at the violin, he knew that he did not have the level of passion required in music to make it his life's work. As he explored his own quest to discover what work he would find fulfilling, he discovered a personal fascination about people together with an innate desire to solve problems. He realized that the combination of these two elements could be powerful and motivating for him. For the last 30 years Ben has been coaching leaders, entrepreneurs, and the next generation, advocating the importance of doing what you love and loving what you do.

Sophie's story and the motivation behind wanting to join Ben in writing this book came later in life. Her attitude to work has been 'stripey' across her career, a mix of deep joy and abject frustration at different times. Having worked inside big multinationals (Coca-Cola and Procter & Gamble), worked with other companies when agency side and a consultant, she also set up, ran and sold her own business. The experiences of working as a founder-entrepreneur, working in client-facing roles and working in big multinationals were very different, and the culture of the organizations where she worked varied wildly. Across that time she had moments of being passionately, deeply in love, motivated and buoyant at work. She also had other periods of feeling heartbroken or trapped in a relationship she couldn't change. Working with, mentoring and coaching others, she has also seen the patterns of work for them and what a difference it can make to pause and consider what could (and should) be done to improve or change habits and approaches. The drive for us to write this book was simple: to make it quicker and easier for others to do what they love, and love what they do.

A few years ago, both of us came to an important revelation in the work that we were doing. We recognised the power of sharing stories to help accelerate learning. We'd both been taking quite a classic approach to coaching and business. This changed when we were given feedback from people we were working with. They repeatedly asked us to share more stories. They wanted to learn from real scenarios, from the tales and experiences others had faced. Stories help make principles real and help learning be more accessible, relatable and (importantly) memorable. Stories make connections. So this book is also a great way for us to share some examples from real-life learning; stories of the struggles and the successes of others who have found ways to love work more.

About you: Moving up, moving on, moving faster

This book is for you if you're moving *up* through your work, moving *on to* a new role or simply want to move *faster* and go *further*. We will be exploring some of the possible situations you might find yourself in:

- Like love relationships, work relationships sometimes need to come to an end. But sometimes that's either not possible or practical (when you are the founder of a business and have others relying on you, for example). Running away is often not the grown-up, sensible approach, and sometimes it can mean that you miss out on opportunities for a renaissance in your work experience.
- You have realized that work can be done in different ways (and in different places), and this has spurred you on to want to embrace more dynamic ways of working to help you do your best work.
- You want to make your work more meaningful and memorable. You know it's possible to combine your vision and skills and to stand for something more than a position or a role.
- As things evolve rapidly and dramatically in the dynamic world of work, you want to be at the forefront of change.

Working on your relationship with work can be transformative. The energy of the satisfaction of doing work well (and work treating you well) can be a gamechanger that can alter your whole life.

Whatever your situation, we hope you find this book digestible, accessible and enjoyable to read – and that it helps. We want to stimulate your curiosity and to believe that doing what you love and loving what you do can be possible. We want to provide you with the shortcuts to get you there.

About the book

LoveWork is a crystallization of both our experience and the experience of others we have spoken to as research for this book. Our main analysis has been among those seen as white-collar workers, those who, in various forms, work in offices, with people and with businesses. Alongside this we have conducted in-depth interviews with a range of people in academia, entrepreneurs and those in C-suite roles across a variety of sectors including aviation, banking, FMCG, hospitality, insurance, legal, medical, property, retail, technology and transportation.

By synthesizing key insights and referencing relevant research, we have created a powerful model for you to use. There are three pivotal stages in the process and across those, seven tangible steps to follow. To thrive in the workplace, you need to discover, develop, and then deliver your own ways to LoveWork more.

Stage 1: (Discover) This provides the analysis and insight to create the foundation of self-knowledge.

Stage 2: (Develop) is the opportunity for you to test and challenge your thinking to expand your impact and influence.

Stage 3 (Deliver) enables you to apply and iterate your approach to make work consistently better.

Here's a high-level overview of the Seven Steps that make up the 3D Model which will help you LoveWork.

Stage One – Discover

Find your fuel invites you to define your purpose, that is, your reason for existence. In the absence of having a clear 'why', you are at risk of following others' agendas, or being distracted by external factors which take you away from your 'true north'. Everyone has a purpose, but most people haven't stopped long enough to discover it. Without a clearly articulated purpose it is difficult to be deliberate about doing the work you love and loving the work you do. Once you find your fuel, it will help you with defining your priorities, making your big decisions and driving you to help make the world a better place.

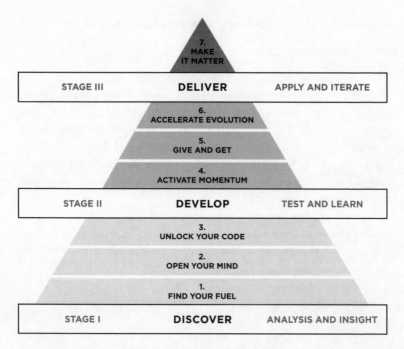

The 3D LoveWork Model™

Open your mind challenges you to connect with the vision to do the work you love and love the work you do. All great ideas start with inspiration, an insight, a eureka moment which leads you to create a compelling picture of a desired future. Opening your mind allows you to explore what inspires you; it is about the art of possibility and transforming your work into something you love.

Unlock your code enables you to take a stand for what you believe is right. It is an act of courage to do what you love and love what you do because it may challenge others' assumptions. Identifying crucible moments that have shaped who you are helps you find your compass. Using that compass then means you are in a more powerful position to navigate the path to where you want to go.

Stage Two – Develop

Activate momentum encourages you to unlock the potential for doing the work you love by overcoming roadblocks that could get in the way. This includes putting an emphasis on playing to your strengths, being in a state of flow and developing your capability. It helps you flourish and progress at pace.

Give and get reminds us that relationships are at the heart of work. The quality of them determines the quality of our work. The majority of people fail to prioritize relationships in ways that enhances their work. Too often people make relationships a by-product of task. We need to understand that partnerships are the essence of getting things done. At the core of give and get is trust. Trust is the glue that secures the connections which enable us to do what we love.

Accelerate evolution urges you to adapt at pace. This is essential in ongoing times of change, complexity, ambiguity and uncertainty. Nobody can predict the future. Nobody has the whole set of answers to what's going on. There is no 'new normal' for how to work. The rule book has been thrown away. We have to work in real time, sometimes moment to moment, and this requires a learning mindset fuelled by intense curiosity. The future will be led by those who stay hungry and adapt the quickest. Being curious, nimble and flexible will enable you to thrive on the velocity of change that characterizes our environment. Simply put, if you don't accelerate your evolution, the opportunity to do the work you love will be limited.

Stage Three – Deliver

Make it matter recognizes that so many of us believe that life is too short to do work that doesn't make a positive difference. After discovering and developing the self-knowledge and skills you need, how do you deliver in a way which creates impact? The motive to make work meaningful is an intrinsic human need. What's important is to be clear about the type of difference you want to make. For many, the point of work is to help the next generation be better equipped to solve problems or to leave the world a better place. Working out how to deliver that enables you to be on the path to make a real impact and a significant difference.

LoveWork is structured to make reading it as digestible as possible. Each chapter breaks down into a few big ideas. At the end of each idea there is a 'Lovenote' to nudge you forward. Every chapter concludes with an 'At the heart of it', which is a short summary for those who like to keep it simple. Throughout the book we have included the *LoveWork* model and toolkit which give you the methodology to put *LoveWork* into action.

The ultimate question at the core of this is: if you don't chart your path to do the work you love, then who will? You are the one who can actively improve your relationship with your work; we're here to help show you ways to do that. Follow the *LoveWork* formula to discover a critical component of what you are going to do with your precious life. Don't just survive at work; work out how to thrive – and be fully alive in those 90,000 hours.

STAGE I

Discover

Welcome to the first, foundational phase of resetting your relationship with work: the Discovery Stage. Here you will find an invitation to give yourself some 'time to think'. Together we will explore the answers to the critical 'why', 'what' and 'how' questions that will enable you to evolve your work. This is a moment for individual reflection and analysis which some might find uncomfortable or challenging but which nonetheless provides a powerful opportunity to uncover the truth and the reality of how you work (and how you respond to work).

Without this self-knowledge it's harder and more complicated to find a rewarding relationship with work. We will guide you all the way, using examples, stories and perspectives to make this journey of discovery as relevant and as enjoyable as possible. This important first stage helps you dig deep to build firm foundations for a bright future.

I
Find your fuel

Why work?

We have been plagued by this question for years. We wanted to know the real reason for work. On the outside there is a range of factors from money to self-actualization. Other elements include interest, learning, challenge, status, power, identity, credibility, contribution and meaning.

What we found in our early inquiry was that the majority of people we coached had no clear definition of what work meant to them. They were not able to explain why they did it, or how to navigate the multiple drivers for their satisfaction and choices at work.

> In the absence of a clear and compelling reason for work,
> your life will be driven by external influences.

Wayne was a case in point. Approaching 50, he had achieved beyond his expectations. As Chief Financial Officer for a tech company, he was at the forefront of a fast-moving and game-changing business. On paper he had an exciting role and was a story of success. However, when we sat down to discuss why he was interested in coaching he rapidly revealed that he was unhappy in his work. He felt frustrated by the feeling of being trapped on a corporate treadmill. The demands of the business left him with little time to think strategically, invest in people and provide the quality of service he aspired to.

We asked him about his definition of work. It was rooted in his family of origin and was out of date. Wayne's grandfather had been a miner working down the pits. His father was a professional footballer whose playing career was cut short by injury. He then retrained as a plumber. The primary message he had taken from his male lineage was 'work hard to pay the bills'. Wayne followed suit and played it safe. He trained in accountancy, working his way up the corporate ladder through long hours to keep shareholders satisfied. In 30 years of work, he had never stepped back to question its meaning.

We asked him why he worked. Wayne's response focused on provision of wealth creation for his family and executive progression. Understandable, but not exactly a compelling proposition. We asked him to dig deeper and think about what work offered beyond security and status. On more considered reflection, Wayne identified the following measures:

- unlocking personal potential
- learning and development
- solving problems
- making change happen
- helping others grow
- developing meaningful relationships
- adding value.

We challenged him to consider what it would be like if this became his work reality. Wayne got curious. He began to see the potential impact of seeing work differently.

Before changing your work, change your definition of work.

We encouraged him to apply his new work measures every day. Wayne agreed to start his morning looking through a different lens, before jumping straight into email and meetings. He focused on some simple questions to reframe his current approach:

4

How can I stretch my potential?

What can I learn and develop?

What is the big problem to solve that is the best use of my time?

How can I drive change for the better?

Who can I help grow?

What relationships should I cultivate?

What is the real value I can add?

Applying these types of questions stimulated his brain agility. Neuroscientist Tara Swart explains: 'Reframing your current approach to situations … can help maximize the brain's performance across diverse and unfamiliar tasks' (Swart, 2018).

Over time Wayne formed a different relationship with work. Redefining what it meant to him ensured that he showed up with a changed mindset. As Wayne moved away from seeing work as a means to an end, he became immersed in the multiple opportunities that work offers. He became fascinated in human potential and how to unlock it. He gave more time to solving the significant issues the company faced. This took him into new areas such as innovation and customer experience. Wayne's new approach was remarkable enough to capture the attention of others. His CEO wanted to know what had happened! He gave glowing feedback to Wayne on his renewed engagement and the positive impact it was having across the organization.

We have observed this type of dramatic shift on many occasions. When individuals move from a fixed position about work (formed by their past) to a more compelling way of thinking about why they work, it leads to a transformation in energy.

In our interview with John Holland-Kaye, CEO, Heathrow, he shared: 'The most fulfilling times in my work are when I find meaning. This occurs when I have thrown myself into what I'm doing because there is the opportunity to hook on to things of real value which go beyond financial matters.' He went on to describe how, on entering the workplace, he quickly discovered that the people who did the best were not necessarily those who went to the 'top' schools:

> Work gave many people the opportunity to fulfil their potential which had not been nurtured by our educational system. I came to believe that it doesn't matter where you have come from because what matters is where you are going. This shaped my belief that my primary role in work is to help people unlock their talent and to achieve where they want to go.

Jonathan Mills, CEO of Choice Hotels Europe, shared his reflections on the role of work:

> There are a couple of lenses to look through when questioning the value of your work. Firstly look at the stage of your work evolution. For instance, for those who have been working for a length of time, do you have a different perspective now from when you first started out at work? Reflect upon the love factor when you started work. If it has diminished, is there a way to reignite it? Secondly, look at the type of work you are doing and consider the impact it has on you subject to your job, career, industry and where you are on your work path. I believe that loving your work is relevant to any type of job and in any industry. However, there has to be a passion for what you do, whether it's connected to the type of work, the environment in which you work, or the tangible difference you are making through delivery. Passion needs to be at the core of why you are working in order to love your work.

To find your fuel, reflect on your primary reasons for work. The way in which Keith Barr, CEO of InterContinental Hotels Group, expressed this resonated with us: 'Don't chase a title, or money. Chase the work you love and the way you want to work.' He went on to say: 'Find out what you love to do and how you love to work. For instance, some people like working for small companies, others for big companies and others in entrepreneurial environments.'

Graham Alexander, Founder of The Alexander Partnership, backed this up: 'There is nothing more important than finding the work you love and making money at it!' He added:

> To find the work you love you need to get in touch at a deep level within yourself and discover the spark that provides the possibility of loving what you do. Ask yourself the big question 'What do you want your work to be about?' Make sure you answer from your heart, not just your head.

Lovenote

Craft your definition of work so you love it. Choose words that are personal and meaningful for you. Why do you work?

Start with purpose

At the time of writing this, we are in the foothills of COVID-19. We know that everyone's lives will change in ways that we cannot yet fully comprehend. The implications will be likely to include:

- the health impact of physical illness (including mortality) as well as the mental health impact of isolation, anxiety and fear (World Health Organization, 2020)
- the economic disruption across the world (Reeves, Carlsson-Szlezak and Swartz, 2020)
- the social impact of enhanced capacity and flexible deployment of staff, easing of legislative and regulatory requirements, containing/slowing the virus and managing the deceased (Department of Health and Social Care, 2020).

In the face of this global crisis, for some people to focus on individual purpose seems to have little point. We would argue the opposite. The idea of purpose has come of age and is needed now more than ever. Uncertainty, ambiguity and unpredictability are running higher than at any point in living memory. So amid all that, what is it that anchors you? Where is your certainty or your internal compass which guides where you want to go? What sustains you beyond survival? Purpose is your reason for existence. It is the essence of who you are and why you do what you do. Purpose provides an aspirational reason for being. It is a deep conviction about what is most important for you. And purpose shapes your mindset, providing the ultimate filter for decision making. This speeds up and simplifies how you should move forward. Think of it as the light which illuminates the brightest path open to you.

8

> Purpose is the key ingredient that fuels you.

There has been a significant corporate gearchange which has implications for all those exploring the impact of their work. The business world has seen a seismic shift towards businesses focused on finding purpose beyond profit. Forty-one per cent of Fortune 500 CEOs, when polled by *Fortune* magazine in March 2019, said that solving social problems should be 'part of their core business strategy'.

Four months later, a survey by New Paradigm Strategy Group, for the same magazine, noted that 64 per cent of Americans agreed with the statement that a company's 'primary purpose' should be to 'make the world better'. Then, in August 2019, the Business Roundtable in the USA announced a new purpose for the corporation, throwing the old one into the garbage. Its new statement is 300 words long. It is only on word 250 that it refers to 'shareholders'. Before that, the group talks about creating 'value for customers, investing in employees, fostering diversity and inclusion, dealing fairly and ethically with suppliers, supporting the communities in which we work and protecting the environment'.

From a more personal perspective Bill Gates is passionate about purpose and has referenced it repeatedly over the years. In 2001 Gates's good friend Warren Buffett invited him to speak to a group of business leaders about what he and his wife, Melinda, were learning on their foundation trips. 'I was energized while speaking about global health,' Gates recalls. It was 'the day I knew what I wanted to do for the rest of my life' (quoted in Elkins, 2019).

Another lens of purpose comes from one of Ben's past school companions, Daniel Hope, who recounts in an interview for *The Guardian* newspaper how Yehudi Menuhin once told him: 'One has to play every day. One is like a bird, and can you imagine a bird saying, "I'm tired today – I don't feel like flying"?'

In Oprah Winfrey's book *The Path Made Clear* (2017), the media mogul describes the moment she discovered her purpose. It was August 1978, and she was working as a news anchor and reporter on *People Are Talking*, a Baltimore talk show – but it didn't feel right. 'I knew I was not my authentic self,' she writes. 'And my bosses certainly made no secret of their feelings. They told me I was the wrong colour, the wrong size, and that I showed too much emotion.' Despite never being 'fully comfortable' covering the six o'clock news, the job led her to an early 'aha' moment. When she was 'demoted' to co-host, she said she 'experienced the first spark of what it means to become fully alive'. While interviewing soap opera actor Tom Carvel (of Carvel ice cream fame) on the show, she 'felt lit up from inside, like I had come home to myself … I was energized in a way that fuelled every cell of my being'. She goes on to impart one of the many lessons that emerge from her book. 'Your life is not static. Every decision, setback, or triumph is an opportunity to identify the seeds of truth that make you the wondrous human being that you are,' she writes. 'I'm not talking just about what you do for a living. When you pay attention to what feeds your energy, you move in the direction of the life for which you were intended.'

We believe that part of your life's journey is to discover your purpose and your life's joy is to live it. Why? Because you will connect with your truth about what is most important, most meaningful and most significant to you. Once you have clarity about your purpose, you are in an authentic position to shape your work, life and relationships accordingly. We resonated with the way Brian Woodhead, Customer Service Director of Transport for London, talked about his why: 'Everything flows when your work is based on a mix of having a clear sense of purpose, doing what inspires you and generating positive energy.'

In 2005 Ben was asked to work with Andy Cosslett when he became the CEO for InterContinental Hotels Group. In partnership with Tracy Robbins, Executive Vice President of Human Resources, Andy had created a core purpose for the company – 'Great Hotels Guests Love' – and wanted to develop purpose-led leaders. Ben remembers sitting in Tracy's office to discuss the creation of a leadership programme in the area of purpose. He was not an expert on purpose at the time so was somewhat nervous; however, the idea gripped him. Over the next 12 years he was fortunate to help more than a thousand leaders globally within the company to discover and to lead with purpose. This experience shaped his credentials for developing purpose in others, which has become instrumental to the expression of his own purpose.

> The most important factor in doing what you love and loving what you do is to understand your own purpose and to let it fuel your work.

So how do you find your purpose? The discovery of personal purpose requires willingness, open-mindedness and an intense curiosity. It is a reflective process supported by some simple but soul-searching steps that allow clarity to emerge. Those of you who thrive on logic, quick thinking and making snap judgements will need to suspend your typical thinking. Purpose emanates from your head, heart and guts. The process may also be influenced by how you process information. For instance, you may be more of a visual learner and access reflections through visual images; you might be more of a kinaesthetic learner where you will learn through experience; or your preference might be through talking and listening as an auditory learner. Whatever your preference, you will need to set aside time to focus and follow these three fundamental steps:

- **Step 1** requires you to identify peak experiences or moments that have had the biggest impact on you. Think about when you have been at your best, in flow, energized and truly fulfilled. What was going on? What was the experience? What was happening? Let's use Ben as our example here. Ben's peak experiences include:
  - *Playing football.* When he was growing up, his dream was to become a professional footballer and in particular to play for his boyhood team, Leeds United. He was never happier than when playing football.

- ○ *Travelling.* After leaving the music world, Ben travelled. One moment stands out when he went to live in Israel on a kibbutz in the Negev Desert. He arrived in Tel Aviv in early January having left a cold and wet England. He had a few hours before his bus so he went and sat on the beach overlooking the Mediterranean Sea. He was transported into a different world.
- ○ *Writing.* Ben wasn't a big fan of writing in formal education. However, once he stumbled into the world of personal development, one of his goals was to write a book. One of his proudest moments was getting his first book contract. He had no idea how he would write it, but he knew that it was the right thing to do and that it would evolve.
- **Step 2** requires you to identify the key themes that you associate with each experience and to understand why they were so meaningful for you. Why were they so significant? What impact did they have? What are the big themes relevant to your purpose? Continuing with the exploration of Ben's purpose, his big themes were:
- ○ *Passion.* Football unleashed his energy. Ben recognizes that unless he is truly passionate about something, then he is not 'on purpose'.
- ○ *Freedom.* Travel connects Ben with a sense of adventure and freedom which are fundamental to his wellbeing.
- ○ *Creativity.* Writing accesses learning and creativity, which are essential ingredients for his fulfilment.
- **Step 3** requires you to reflect deeply about what these themes have in common and why they are so significant for you by asking questions such as:

> What is your passion?

> What matters most?

> What is most meaningful?

> What difference do you want to make?

> What value do you want to add?

In Ben's case, the insight that emerged from exploring these questions was the importance of *truth*. Ben has always been driven to understand what is true and real. Ben describes his purpose as 'being an enabler of truth'. The translation of this into work is to develop 'better leaders for a better world'. In other words, he is passionate about creating the conditions for others to discover what is true for them and to help make the world a better place.

To find your purpose take the following three steps:

Step 1 *Identify peak moments or memorable chapters when you have been in flow*	Step 2 *Identify key themes associated with each moment or chapter and why they were so meaningful*	Step 3 *Recognize the links between your big themes to help define your purpose*
When have I been at my best? What was happening when I experienced peak experiences? When have I been most energized? When have I been truly fulfilled?	Why did these experiences mean so much to me? Why were they so significant? What impact did they have? What are the big themes relevant to my purpose?	What have my themes got in common? What is most meaningful for me? What difference do I want to make? What legacy do I want to leave?

To stimulate your own exploration, here are some example answers given by clients as they sought to discover their purpose:

Client	Step 1 *Identify peak moments or memorable chapters when you have been in flow*	Step 2 *Identify key themes associated with each moment or chapter and why they were so meaningful*	Step 3 *Recognize the links between your big themes to help define your purpose*
John	Racing fast cars Leading turnarounds in companies Building high-performing teams	Speed Change Partnership	*Link:* Making change happen in a dynamic way through people *Purpose:* To be a creator of opportunity

Suzanne	Developing others Delivering big projects Presenting ideas	Growth Achievement Innovation	*Link:* Making progress in creative ways *Purpose:* To achieve the impossible
Brian	Unlocking potential Working collaboratively Having children	Possibility Team Learning	*Link:* Learning how to unlock the potential of people and projects *Purpose:* To be a maximizer
Carmen	Playing to strengths Completing big transactions Living in different countries	Energy Challenge Culture	*Link:* Being challenged to adapt and grow *Purpose:* To realize potential
Grant	Competing in endurance sports Mentoring others Starting up new business	Winning Helping Risk	*Link:* Taking risk to win and help others along the way *Purpose:* To be the best I can be

The following are some of the frequently asked questions we are asked in the quest for purpose:

- **How do I know if I have found my purpose?** Some of the tell-tale signs include having a strong emotional connection with the insight that emerges; having a sense of coming home to a truth you already know; being intellectually stimulated by the idea; being internally motivated by the concept and being inspired to follow it.
- **Does my purpose have to be a pithy statement?** No. What we encourage you to do is to connect with the meaning of the words that emerge, rather than overthink them.

- **Is simplicity good?** We are big advocates of simplifying complexity. For instance, we have coached people who arrived at things like love and happiness as a purpose but thought it was too simplistic. However, these are some of life's biggest goals for many – simple but essential. The key in those cases was not rejecting these as 'too obvious' but instead articulating exactly what they meant for the individuals concerned.

- **Will my purpose change?** Our humble point of view is that, no, it won't if you have already arrived at your core 'truth'. What does change, however, is the application of purpose throughout the various stages of your life. For instance, how your purpose impacts family will fluctuate subject to what's going on in your family situation. How your purpose translates at work will change subject to different stages and requirements.

- **Is purpose linked to circumstance?** We believe that purpose transcends circumstance and that one way of knowing if you are on purpose or not is the consistency of it beyond changing circumstances.

Finding your purpose is not always a quick or easy process. It requires reflection but it is an essential part of your journey. Errol Williams, Vice President at WeWork, shared his experience of prioritizing purpose: 'In deciding the work I love to do my primary consideration has been to find a sense of purpose. I ask myself, "Is there meaning in this work? Is there something really good in this work?"'

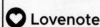 **Lovenote**

Purpose is your big why. Discover it, live it, thrive.

The perfect match

In our interview with Emma Gilthorpe, COO, Heathrow, she described her experience starting at the company and how her sense of purpose and work united:

> The first time I really noticed my deep-rooted love for what I did was when I arrived Heathrow. Prior to that I had been working in telecommunications for 15 years. I genuinely enjoyed what I did there, but after a few months at Heathrow I realised that this was different. I experienced more excitement, more energy, more focus. I could see I was making a tangible difference day-to-day through my actions – for passengers, airlines and colleagues – creating a fresh sense of fulfilment.

We believe life is too short to not love what you do. What if your work was an expression of your purpose? What if your purpose and work connected in ways you haven't yet considered? Having a clear purpose guides your work and becomes the fuel to run on. In our conversation with Graham Alexander, Founder of The Alexander Partnership, he gave his advice about purpose:

> Find something that captivates you … Follow what you love with such a passion and then find a way to make money out of it. Discovering your purpose can point you in the direction of the work you love. You can then assess opportunities against your sense of purpose. If you are working in an organization, make sure it is aligned with what you are passionate about. The holy grail is to find ways of getting close to doing 100 per cent of what you love and that adds value to a business.

Siân Evans, Director of Leadership and Colleague Experience at Simplyhealth, had a powerful experience about bringing work and purpose together: 'The catalyst for me to realize that I had a choice about doing the work I love was burnout.' While she was unwell, she focused on her work and through a process of reflection knew that she had 'a deep passion to help other people get to know who they are'. Siân recognized that she needed to do the things that energized her as well as thinking about the legacy she wanted to leave:

> I was working in Human Resources at the time and wanted to be known for something more than being good at doing restructures and redundancies! I wanted to do something that had a purpose and made a difference to other people. I followed my passion about developing people and wanting to help unlock their potential. I went back into work wanting to get involved in leadership and management development. Fortunately, I worked for an exceptional manager who unlocked doors for me to make it happen. I learned that once you are awake you can never go back to sleep. When I discovered what I loved there was no going back.

We are wary of making it appear too easy or simplistic to integrate purpose and work. It usually requires a 'wake-up' call in the form of a setback, failure or frustration to get people's attention. We have observed a range of occasions including firings, business failures and relationship challenges which have turned people to asking why they do what they do, how they could do things differently and what role purpose plays.

Liam was a highly ambitious property development director in a global company. The organizational structure had various executive levels and Liam was a Vice President waiting for the haloed promotion to Senior Vice President. We had been coaching Liam for a couple of months when a peer of his succeeded in gaining a promotion to Senior Vice President ahead of him. Liam was ready to throw in the towel as the peer was younger and he thought he was ahead in the pecking order. We got to Liam just in time before he handed in his resignation and challenged him to use the experience as a work-defining moment. What if, rather than fixating on a title, he utilized the disappointment as a reason to dig deep, discover his purpose and see his work differently?

Liam was willing to experiment. He spent the next few weeks exploring his purpose. We challenged him to reflect on when he was at his best, energized and fulfilled in his work and life. Some of the activities that got Liam in the zone included:

- being out on his mountain bike – he loved nature and pitting his wits against rough terrain
- supporting his children as they grew up and helping them overcome all the obstacles that young people face, from educational challenges to relationship problems
- guiding his clients to land big deals that supported their business growth while hitting his own targets
- developing a cohesive team that worked together as a well-oiled machine
- contributing to his charity of choice, helping people fight bad housing or homelessness on their own.

Through his reflections Liam alighted on some meaningful themes such as creating possibility, simplifying complexity, helping others and experiencing freedom. He distilled these into the essence of his purpose: 'To inspire others to be free and fulfilled.' We challenged Liam to look at his work through the lens of purpose. What would it be like to commit to a purpose, not a position? What would it mean to focus on being purpose-led rather than to be led by a title? What would be different if he chose a purpose, rather than a job?

> Letting your work be an expression of your purpose is a game-changer.

These were new questions for Liam, but he was willing to embrace them. We coached him to step back and map out what his work could look like based on purpose. He came up with the following overview:

To inspire others to be free and fulfilled			
My success criteria	1. Make work an expression of purpose	2. Develop a purpose-led team	3. Drive sustainable growth

My priorities	Inspire self	Align the team	Create a great
	Inspire others	to lead with	place to work
	Do inspired	purpose	Balance
	work	Engage	purpose and
		stakeholders	profit
		through	Champion
		purpose	business as a
		Accelerate	force for good
		performance	
		with purpose	

This picture was completely different from Liam's previous measure of work, which was primarily focused on delivering financial targets, satisfying customer needs and seeking the next promotion. Liam shared the impact that the discovery of his purpose had on him. He realized that he had never taken the opportunity to rethink work. From early on in his career he had simply focused on climbing as high as he could go, as quickly as possible. Despite his success, however, he felt 'there was something missing':

Finding my purpose was the missing piece. Once I started exploring my purpose there was no going back. It was as if I unlocked a tidal wave of passion and energy that had been misdirected. Thinking about work differently was liberating. Understanding that I could give work a new meaning was a revelation. It was such a simple yet profound concept …

I recognized that in order to inspire others I needed to be inspired myself. I started to focus on what inspired me and what switched me off. I challenged myself to be more inspired on a daily basis. This was a different experience than simply trying to tick off my 'to do' list as quickly as possible. I became energized. I reconnected with the activist in me that wanted to make the world a better place but had become worn down and disillusioned with corporate dynamics. I needed to take another level of ownership about the creation of my work and the value I added.

Liam also began to see the value of purpose, not just for himself, but for his whole team. He started to have conversations with his team, gradually introducing them to the idea of purpose and discussing what it could be like to be purpose-led. He discovered there was a genuine appetite to have a shared purpose and engage others in a different way. This translated itself into the team's performance as it broadened its focus to not just *what* it was achieving, but *why* and *how* it was doing it: 'Ultimately, we wanted it to stick and so we baked our purpose into our business approach including how we recruited and developed people, managed performance, adapted critical processes, communicated and made product and financial decisions.'

Liam's discovery and espousal of purpose ultimately also had an impact on his career:

I look back and appreciate the catalyst that missing out on the promotion provided. Coincidentally an opportunity to step in to an SVP role emerged about six months later, and this time I approached it differently. My narrative focused on what I could give and the difference I could make. I was successful in gaining the role, but my reaction surprised me. My excitement now lay in the fact that I could expand my purpose, rather than puff my chest out with the pride of a new title. I genuinely now define my work as an opportunity to inspire others to be free and fulfilled, which is putting my purpose into action.

Someone who has had an innate sense of purpose and has challenged herself to blend it with her work from an early age is Sam Barrell, COO of the Francis Crick Institute. In our conversation she shared how from a young age she had felt a strong vocation to become a doctor:

It was my choice to do medicine and I fought hard to make it a reality. I found the study of it totally fascinating … and I graduated feeling totally inspired to begin my career as a doctor. I worked crazy hours but loved it. I found it purpose-led, high challenge, stimulating, incredibly hard work and totally fulfilling. [Even today] I am always acquiring new knowledge and growing as a person, whilst retaining that strong sense of central purpose. Working in teams with people who inspire you and who share a common purpose is an incredible feeling – it's the lifeblood that motivates you to make things better for people.

She took her sense of purpose into her new position at the Francis Crick Institute: 'My career is still tethered to the central thread of helping people live better lives. Every moment of the day is different which I thrive on, and I am enriched by the constant challenges and by working with highly talented and engaging people.'

Someone else who prioritizes matching purpose and work is Nick Dent, Director Customer Operations at London Underground. In our interview he stated: 'I work in jobs and organizations which I enjoy. Period. Why? Because it's essential to be happy in order to excel, do your best work and be the best you can be. I have done jobs that I didn't enjoy and as a result I was not successful.' He also clarified the importance of purpose, which, in a role as challenging as keeping London moving, is vital: 'I need to have a clear and exciting purpose that gets me out of bed. It's vital that I can see the relationship between what I do, what my team does and how it flows back to purpose.' Your work can be an expression of your purpose and become your fuel. However, you need to be deliberate about it.

♥ Lovenote

Purpose is the fuel to spark a better relationship with work.

Making a commitment

Once you've had the 'wake-up' call about the power of purpose and aligning it with your work, you need to make it stick. Staynton Brown, Director of Diversity and Inclusion at Transport for London, recounts how, early on, he made a vow to himself:

> When I left university, I went into a marketing and sales role. It was one of the most informative points in my career. I was doing what I thought graduates should do. Securing a role and earning a reasonable amount. However, the work I was doing didn't make my heart sing. It was in the financial sector and the outcome of my work was actually getting poor people into more debt. I became very low and felt heavy. At that point I vowed I would never do anything again that wouldn't help the world become a better place.

The joy he expresses regarding his sense of purpose in his current work is inspirational:

> I want to make sure that whatever I do makes my soul sing and my heart go into rapture. The work I do has to be purpose-led. I need to feel that the work I do has a bigger cause beyond myself. My why is making sure I contribute to healthier and better communities, break down barriers and help people live a good life.

What vow have you made about work? What is your normal mindset for work? What do you focus on? Where do you put your attention? Neuroscientists estimate that, on the unconscious level, the human brain can process roughly 11 million pieces of information per second. Compare that to the estimate for conscious processing: about 40 pieces per second (DiSalvo, 2013). As a result, the brain creates mental shortcuts to help us interpret information faster and save energy in making decisions. We rely on our past experiences to do this, and, when faced with similar situations or people, we automatically make associations. A study from the Research Centre based at UCL Epidemiology and Public Health shows that on average it takes 66 days to set ourselves up to form new patterns of behaviour, at which point we reach a limit of self-reported automaticity for performing an initially new behaviour (Lally, 2009). Therefore, to follow your purpose means that you need to make it a conscious choice and stick to it relentlessly in order to form a new habit.

On a regular day, what is on your mind on waking? What are the formative thoughts you have and the initial decisions you make? Our mind usually slips straight into autopilot as we contemplate the day ahead in the form of a 'to do' list. We automatically think about the tasks to complete including actions to take, places to be, people to meet, conversations to hold, emails to manage and food to eat. Not the most inspiring of lists. What if, instead, we started the day with reflections on purpose? What if we developed a habit where our waking thoughts were focused on our purpose through work? For instance, if your purpose hinges on making a difference, then your morning focus could be:

What kind of difference do I want to make today?

How can my work make a difference?

How can I help others make a difference?

If your purpose is connected with a sense of possibility, then your focus could be:

> What is possible today?

> How can my work create new possibilities for the better?

> How can I help others create new possibilities?

Shift your mindset from 'What have I got to do today?' to 'How can I be purpose-led?' This change could become one of the most important steps you take to integrate your reason for being with your work. It means that you start the day by moving from an unconscious reaction to a conscious choice. It will set you up for a very different reality.

Every day let your purpose fuel your work.

Staynton Brown reflected on this when he remarked:

As life changes you need to keep checking in. Ask yourself what is my purpose, what is my why? Is what you are doing making your soul sing? Make sure you don't atrophy when you are alive. Be really honest with yourself. We're not always honest with ourselves about what we really care about. It means that you will need to dig deep and do some soul searching. Draw upon people you trust, or who have a different take on the world to challenge your thinking. It's important to acknowledge the wider social expectations placed on you and to be honest about what drives you.

Our mindset has been wired in a way that we tend to tell ourselves, 'When we *have* what we think we want, we will *do* the things we want to do and *be* the type of person we want to be.' This is backward thinking. We need to adopt the paradigm: '*Be* the person you want to be to inspire the things you want to *do* which will shape the outcomes you *have*.' From a purpose perspective this means developing the following mindset: *be* purpose-led to fuel the things you want to *do* which will shape the outcomes you *have*.

Another way of making purpose stick was expressed by Errol Williams, Vice President at WeWork:

> We get up every day and put in 10–14 hours of our time to work. Therefore we might as well choose to love our work because, even if we're doing it to make ends meet, we're still putting in the hours. When you love and enjoy your work is when your natural talents tick. For instance, there are people who love to serve others and become teachers or social workers. There are those who love to solve problems who become consultants. You have others who love to create things and become designers. It's important to line up your work with your intrinsic wiring so that your real self becomes activated.

Once you have clarity about your purpose, write down each day how you want to be purpose-led. Don't operate on autopilot. Make it tangible so that you can measure the impact of it during the day:

- Notice the difference it makes to your energy, curiosity, drive and inspiration.
- See how it can lift you up from being in a mode of transaction to a space of transformation.
- Observe how it can encourage you to think creatively about the activities in your schedule.
- Watch how it causes you to be present, rather than getting distracted by other things.
- Experience the sense of meaning it gives you about work.

♥ Lovenote

Put purpose into practice every day by matching your 'to be' list with your 'to do' list.

Unite

It was 2012 post the London Olympics. We were fortunate to be asked to coach the Heathrow leadership team responsible for the delivery of Terminal 2, The Queen's Terminal. As John Holland-Kaye, Heathrow CEO, says, 'Heathrow is Hollywood' – in other words, anything related to Heathrow gets high media coverage – so it was critical that the organization got Terminal 2 right. There were some fixed points for the programme – to open on time (4 June 2014) and on budget (£2.4 billion). What was yet to be defined was how the leadership team would work together in order to make it happen.

Brian Woodhead was Terminal 2's Programme and Operations Director. His background was primarily in the commercial sector so opening a terminal in an operational environment was a new experience. We had worked with Brian previously and knew about his passion for building purpose-led teams. In Brian's words:

> I believe it is essential to have a North Star which guides you. The best people I have worked for have been able to set a clear direction and given me the freedom to get on with it. In particular, they focus on the results delivered, not checking the process. My experience shows that when people do not feel empowered or have the autonomy to get on with their work, then it becomes a blocker to their progress.

As a consequence, one of Brian's first acts in role was to schedule a team offsite to define a collective purpose. However, many of the team were Brian's peers with a dotted reporting line and they were busy. The idea of taking 24 hours out of their diaries did not appeal. We had already met with the team on an individual basis ahead of the offsite to get their insights into the current state of the programme and team, and to understand what success would look like going forward. That notwithstanding, when we sat down with the team to debrief the findings, you could have cut the tension in the air with a knife. Some people made it clear that they did not want to be there and thought it was a waste of time.

Unperturbed, Brian summarized the insight from our diagnostic findings, and clearly stated that one of the biggest risks to the terminal opening on time and budget was silo ways of working. He shared his vision for the team, which involved providing inspired leadership, working collaboratively and engaging colleagues to deliver Heathrow's vision 'to give passengers the best airport service in the world'. He laid out the case for having a common purpose over and above hitting the plan. The team began to get curious.

We are used to working in situations where there are varying levels of cynicism about the concept of purpose. Given its intangible nature, there is no surprise that in operational environments people are unsure about the value of defining a common purpose. At Heathrow, we asked the team to adopt an open mind and be prepared to explore the pros and cons of having a shared purpose. It started a healthy debate focused on several factors:

- past experience in work environments with or without a clearly articulated common purpose
- benefits of having collective purpose and risks of transacting without it
- defining a shared purpose for the Terminal 2 delivery programme and the implications thereof if such was agreed.

Some of the comments that arose during discussion of the pros and cons of instigating a shared purpose included:

Pros	Cons
Clear direction and focus over and above the delivery of tangible milestones	Paying lip service to the idea and losing credibility with team members
Creation of a unified culture about 'the way things are done around here'	Failing to hold the team accountable to its pledge
Framework for decision making when faced with difficult trade-offs	Purpose being used as a reason to block decisions if they are uncomfortable

We used a simple process to get under the skin of a shared purpose. We framed it by indicating that it was an exploratory process. This meant not making any immediate usage or implementation decisions. The steps involved asking team members:

1 to generate adjectives to describe why the team existed and what they aspired to be like as a team
2 to select the adjectives, once shared, that had the greatest resonance.

The team came up with multiple adjectives and aligned on some unified themes including growth, inspiration, delivery, people and opportunity. We then challenged the team to create a statement that best represented their intent, and they came up with: 'To inspire people to go beyond what they think is possible'. This statement brought the team together above and beyond the delivery goal. They agreed to call it their 'North Star', pointing them in the direction they needed to travel.

Over the next 18 months we met with the team every three months to review how the team was working together and whether it was staying true to its shared purpose. To make the purpose more tangible, we suggested that the team consider it in relation to a number of elements including:

- **Talent** – aligning the recruitment and development of people to deliver the customer experience they wanted

- **Culture** – creating a consistent set of values and behaviours in order to realize the Heathrow vision and open the terminal on time and on budget
- **Performance management** – setting balanced objectives on what people achieve (delivery metrics), as well as how they achieve them (behaviours)
- **Supply chain** – ensuring supplier values and behaviours were in line with cultural expectations
- **Operations** – adapting processes to align with the purpose
- **Communication** – tailoring internal and external communications to drive engagement consistent with purpose.

It was a career highlight to see the pride in the team when Terminal 2 was officially opened by the Queen on 27 June 2014. About half of the original team were still in role. New people had transitioned over the 18 months in a seamless way into a thriving environment, and the purpose of the team lived on. In March 2018, Terminal 2 was awarded the Best Terminal in the World at the Sky Awards by Skytrax.

> A shared purpose becomes the fuel to move people in the same direction.

Subject to where you are in the formation of an idea, or the development of a team or company, it is vital to engage people in either the co-creation of a purpose, or to be deliberate about how you bring a purpose to life. For instance, as an organization Heathrow has done a remarkable job developing a programme called 'Leading with Purpose and Values', which has rippled to all 6,000 colleagues in various forms, enabling people to authentically connect with the company purpose, 'Making every journey better'. As CEO John Holland-Kaye shared:

One of the most beneficial processes I have done was discovering my personal purpose and values. This involved conducting a timeline exercise when you look back on what has shaped you from your life experience and what matters most to you through the lens of purpose and values. Making sure you are happy with what you are doing is an essential part of having a fulfilled life. At times you will realize that you're in the wrong job or company, at which point it's important to step back and re-evaluate. It is best for you and the company to make sure that it's the right fit and that you are fulfilled in what you are doing.

We have found that you cannot tell people to lead with purpose. You need to provide a safe environment to discover your own personal purpose, explore what it means for you at work and see whether there is the opportunity to make genuine linkages with the company purpose. Organizations need to recognize the risk factor that once they give colleagues the licence to test their own purpose against the company's, some people might choose to leave if they recognize that it's not the right match. Ultimately, this is better for both parties, but it can be a challenging process as it demands trust and transparency from all sides.

On another occasion we supported the hospitality company edyn in the creation of its purpose. The story of edyn is to 'engage and inspire with distinctively designed hotels, firmly rooted in the local neighbourhood and offering vibrant experiences and connections'. Their charismatic CEO, Stephen McCall, is a purpose-driven leader who brought his executive committee together for a two-day retreat to discover the DNA of the company. It was an edgy couple of days: after all, when exploring a shared purpose you never know what answer will emerge. Stephen had rented a country house where we could sit around log fires to contemplate big questions like: 'Why does the company exist?', 'What is its story?' and 'What matters most?' It was essential to create an environment of 'psychological safety', where everyone had share of voice and could speak up. Stephen always sets the right tone by disclosing his own aspirations and vulnerabilities upfront. As he said: 'Specifically I am keen to ensure I have a senior team with a high degree of social awareness, curiosity and a deep affinity with purpose.' He went on to say: 'The meaning of work and the way in which individuals relate to their jobs is changing rapidly, and I need modern, sophisticated leaders to ensure the organization evolves and changes just as quickly.'

Prior to the offsite, the executive committee had brought together a steering group of people passionate about purpose who had engaged nearly half the company through listening groups to give their views about the company purpose. We used this as an input to get the senior team to explore their own ideas through a variety of questions including:

What impact do you want the company to have in the world?

What difference do you want to make?

What legacy do you want to leave?

What do you want to be known for?

How do you want to serve?

Building upon the diverse perspectives of the team including brands, finance, technology, people and operations created rich conversations. What emerged was the purpose: 'Soulful Hospitality'. This resonated on a number of levels through the lens of the four key stakeholder groups (colleague, consumer, customer and community):

- To enable **colleagues** to be human at work and have the opportunity to be their authentic selves and unlock their potential.
- To ensure **consumers** feel valued and recognized as human beings and to experience being truly cared for during their stay.

- To encourage **customers** to build meaningful partnerships and go beyond the transactional nature of supply and demand.
- To engage with local **community** to be part of the company's extended family and benefit from the opportunities created by its ecosystem.

A few weeks later the executive committee invited the top one hundred leaders from the business for the launch of 'Soulful Hospitality'. The event was themed on the original 1969 Woodstock festival, and everyone was invited to dress accordingly! The day gave the wider team the opportunity to become immersed in the DNA of the company and to make a clear choice as to whether they wanted to be part of a soulful future.

Defining and following a shared purpose provides a common identity, a direction to follow, a framework for decision making and a collective sense of meaning. In San Francisco, we are fortunate to work with the iconic brand Ghirardelli, famous for its ice-cream sundaes and irresistible hot fudge sauce. Ghirardelli's core purpose is 'Makes life a bite better', championed by Joel Burrows, their brilliant CEO. Joel has breathed new life into the brand by focusing on what the purpose means for multiple stakeholders. For instance, during the COVID-19 crisis the company did everything in its power to support colleagues and kept the factory open to make chocolate for customers, recognizing that, even in the midst of disaster, a moment of respite in a day can make a positive difference.

Would you want to work for a company or within a team that had no purpose? We doubt it, but in our experience it's surprisingly rare to come across organizations, leaders and teams that engage and fuel people with purpose. For one of our interviewees, the psychologist Amy Edmondson, though, purpose is crucial:

The point of purpose is that we need to have a larger motivation than ourselves. We need purpose as a catalyst for having a greater sense of fulfilment. You might be happy in your work. However, if you don't have the added belief that what you are doing is truly 'worthy', then it's hard to say that you love your work. I like to use the analogy of three bricklayers being asked what they are doing. Bricklayer number 1 says they are laying bricks. Bricklayer number 2 says they are feeding their family. Bricklayer number 3 says they are building a cathedral. Guess who will be most motivated?

For a company that has an existing purpose which truly defines the organization's DNA, make sure that it shows up across the following elements:

- **Talent** – align recruitment, personal and career development with purpose.
- **Culture** – champion and demonstrate desired mindsets and behaviours linked to purpose.
- **Performance** – define metrics and incentivize colleagues on meeting purpose-led targets.
- **Supply chain** – ensure supplier mindsets and behaviours are aligned with the purpose.
- **Communication** – tailor internal and external engagement to purpose.
- **Product** – ensure that the product portfolio reflects the purpose.
- **Capital allocation** – introduce resource in line with purpose-led decisions.

For a company that has not yet defined its purpose, conduct focus groups engaging at least 25 per cent of colleagues with an experiential process to discover the organization DNA. Tap into existing company heritage about the organization origins, cultural heritage and service provision and what makes the company special. Refine insight to align on a unified purpose signed off by the executive committee.

The Standard Hotels is a company fuelled by purpose. In our interview with Amar Lalvani, its charismatic CEO, he discussed the value for an organization of having a shared sense of purpose:

> As we grow around the world, we are hiring individuals who have probably never even been to one of our hotels. Yet they have to live and breathe the brand if we are to deliver what makes The Standard special. Our purpose provides a grounding and a true north. It helps us to educate new team members and to check each other when we go off track. We define our purpose as 'Anything but Standard', which means as a brand we are never complacent. We start projects with a beginner's mind, never rely on industry norms, and are always willing to do things that have never been done before if they improve our guest, community or team experiences.

For a team that has an existing purpose co-created by the majority of team members, use similar elements as illustrated for an organization to bring it to life, as well as ensuring everyone is familiar with each other's personal purpose.

The message is clear: create shared purpose by bringing people together to have a common direction and sense of meaning.

 Lovenote

Unity – and energy – emerges from putting purpose at the heart of everybody and everything you do.

At the heart of it

Formula 1 and other high-octane innovative motorsports constantly push the potential for engine power while staying within the boundaries of the law.

Defining the best super-fuel is so critical an element to success, performance and speed that fuel engineers spend hours and hours getting the right fuel for each engine and each situation.

Take a pitstop in your life. Take a pause to think.

Clarifying why you do what you do is the equivalent of making absolutely sure that you are running on the best, most premium fuel to help you go faster, to thrive and drive forward.

At a very basic level, we all know the danger of putting the wrong fuel in the tank, but, equally, we understand that the power of finding a fuel that is sustainable, that's driven by clean energy or that electrifies can be transformative.

Or, put another way, purpose is like the Powerwall battery which keeps the lights on when the grid goes down.

The steps are as simple as A, B, C:

Articulate it.

Pausing to discover, clarify and then articulate your own purpose is fundamental. Uncovering the truth is essential, but never underestimate the transformative impact of the right language; it should be simple, personal and memorable.

Be it.

It is a conscious, strategic choice to be purpose-led and to put purpose at the heart of your work, relationships and life. Decide to put your purpose into practice at work every day.

Connect it.

This is not just about you. The amplifying impact of unifying difference behind a shared sense of purpose brings direction, energy and momentum.

Finding your fuel accelerates your transition to finding a more sustainable and electrifying way of working.

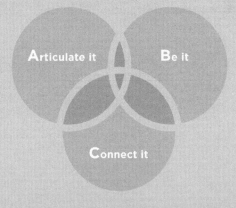

2

Open your mind

Sparks

Does your work excite you? Does it make you want to get out of bed
in the morning? Does it light your fire? Are you working around people
that stimulate you? There is no doubt that you are fortunate if you do
have this type of experience most days, and if not, it's something to go for.
Doing what you love is about your heart and guts, not just your head. It's
about doing what inspires you.

Wise words from David Woodward, former CEO, Heinz Europe, as
he described to us the importance of inspiration at work.

How much is inspiration a key requirement for you?

Scott Barry Kaufman (2011) strongly believes that inspiration, far
from being divine in origin, is within our control – it is, he says, 'an
interaction between your current knowledge and the information
you receive from the world'. As such, 'there are things you can do to
increase the likelihood of inspiration occurring': preparation ('work
mastery'), openness to experience and positive affect being key.

Whatever your experience of inspiration, you can develop it to
become more inspired. However, it will require you to want inspiration, to be intentional about it and to prioritize it. From a personal
perspective, part of the reason we write is to be inspired. Focusing
on 'work mastery' – that is, becoming better at what we do through
expanding our current knowledge and information we receive from
the world – is highly energizing. Writing together challenges us to
think bigger, be open to different experiences and to learn from each

other, and this lifts us up. Interviewing great people is an immediate way of getting inspired by hearing remarkable stories and exploring how to apply lessons learned. The way we write sets us up for small accomplishments along the way as we complete chapters, conduct research and see our ideas evolve.

So what inspires you? Where do you get your inspiration from? Who inspires you? It's essential to step back from your permanent busyness and figure out the role inspiration plays in your work. If you are unclear, then you can't expect others to be able to serve up inspiration on a plate for you. It has to be your own recipe.

Jonathan Mills, CEO EMEA of Choice Hotels, shared the following reflection on inspiration:

> Inspiration comes from a wide range of sources, such as the potential impact that you can have on others, a boss who lifts you up, or a company which recognizes that you are part of an important mix and genuinely values the contribution you make. Being inspired yourself enables you to inspire others which will facilitate a natural love for your work.

Renée Elliott, founder of Planet Organic and co-founder of Beluga Bean, told us how she developed her personal recipe for inspiration:

> Upon graduating in America I came to England and experienced one of my first early shocks – I realized that I was going to have to support myself financially! I felt like nobody had spelled out the fact that I had to earn money. My main skills were in English and communication, so I became a writer. I can clearly remember my first day of work – Monday, 1 September 1986. I sat down at my desk, and the first comment from the guy sitting next to me was 'I can't wait until Friday'. As an optimistic 21-year-old American I saw days, weeks, years stretching out ahead of me. I thought if I'm not inspired by what I do I'll be dead in five years because I'm a passionate person.

After a few years I had the opportunity to go back to the States and attend an intensive personal development programme. I wanted to pursue my interest in spirituality and other possibilities that had been in my awareness. I also planned that I would discover the work I wanted to do and to return to England with a different career. While on the programme it became clear that I wanted to do my own business, to be inspired and to lead others with a cause to get behind. In the local town there was an amazing health food store where I hung out. I observed people in the shop wanting to create a better world. Both employees and customers were committed to living in a more conscious way. It reinforced my belief that I didn't want to do conventional work. From there I went to visit an organic supermarket in my hometown of Boston. I stood in the store and knew this would be my future. The organic movement was all about creating a better world through better farming, eating and living. At the age of 28 I felt that I was getting to know myself.

I went and got the relevant experience and opened Planet Organic at the age of 30 in 1995. The purpose of Planet Organic was twofold. From a purely personal perspective it was an opportunity to create meaningful work that would inspire me. I believe in a life of service and making a difference in the world. From a business perspective my vision was to promote health in the community and an organic supermarket became the vehicle to live the vision and make the world a better place.

Find out what inspires you. What you believe in. What excites you. It is completely possible for work to be a source of inspiration. However, you need to dig deep to know what will get you inspired.

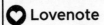 **Lovenote**

To be inspired, know what inspires you.

Painting the picture

At the age of 25 Jonathan had just handed in his notice at the company which had given him his first job in recruitment after coming out of university. He decided to take the plunge to move from an agency to a larger company where he was destined to have a broader role. The day after he informed his employer of his intentions, COVID-19 hit. Unfortunately, the new company withdrew its offer, and his existing employer was not in a position to retain his services. Jonathan was the son of a long-term client of ours and he phoned us in despair. He had been hit by his first major work disappointment and was unsure where to turn. With limited experience he didn't know where he should put his attention. Before he made a reactive decision we encouraged Jonathan to step back and to use the enforced pause caused by COVID to open his horizons. It was time for him to dream and generate a vision.

In our experience it is rare to come across people who have consciously articulated an ideal vision for their work. Yet would you want to work for a company that had no vision? Would you want to follow a leader who had no vision? One person who *has* invested considerable time in painting the picture of their ideal work is Joel Burrows, CEO of Ghirardelli, the iconic chocolate brand in San Francisco. In our interview he told us, 'To thrive at work requires you to have clarity about your bigger picture because if you are too hell bent on achieving one thing you might land up disappointed.' He argues that 'there is a difference between achieving goals and loving your work', and so prioritizes enjoyment over achievement. His number-one priority is being a husband and dad, and while he has always been competitive and wanted to do well in anything he does, it has not been at any cost: 'I know that being sucked into a business that takes everything and leaves me too tired to put my kids to bed is not for me.'

The act of creating a compelling vision is a vital ingredient for doing the work you love and loving the work you do. In our case for vision we have been heavily influenced by the research and insight of Richard Boyatzis, Distinguished Professor at Case Western Reserve University and an Adjunct Professor at the international ESADE

Business School. In his 2019 book *Helping People Change*, co-authored with Melvin Smith and Ellen Van Oosten, he puts forward the power of a personal vision: 'Put simply, a personal vision is an expression of an individual's ideal self and ideal future. It encompasses dreams, values, passions, purpose, sense of calling, and core identity. It represents not just what a person desires to do, but also who she wishes to be.' He and his co-authors ask the reader to consider the following question: 'If your life were ideal (you could substitute *incredible, amazing, awesome*, etc., here) ten to fifteen years from now, what would it be like?' (Boyatzis, Smith and Van Oosten, 2019).

In our interview with Boyatzis, he described how an individual's sense of vision arises: 'Some of the most profound effects on vision originate from our parents, grandparents and early childhood experiences influenced by our culture and faith. Your vision then gets coloured by your teenage experience through friends and social identity pressures which can enhance early learnings about what is a noble life.' From that point on, however, he argues, you can develop your vision. In fact, the process of developing vision became required on the Emotional Intelligence Competency Course he helped set up at the ESADE Business School:

> We spend the first third of the course on vision which requires students to create and write a compelling, comprehensive personal vision statement of their ideal self, which becomes a three to five-page essay. We ask them to cover their dream ten to fifteen years into the future. What does their physical, spiritual, romantic and family health look like? What contribution do they want to make to their community and through their work? We intentionally place work last because we feel that work is a subset of life. If you get work right but not life, it atrophies. If you get life right but not work, you can always change it.

Developing a vision for your life – including your work – enables you to move towards a compelling future. A vision is not a target or strategy. It is not the plan about how you are going to achieve it. Building upon the methodology of Richard Boyatzis and colleagues, ask yourself, 'If your work were ideal (you could substitute *incredible, amazing, great*, etc., here) ten to fifteen years from now, what would it be like?'

Going back to Jonathan (who you will remember was just 25) we asked him to think 15 years ahead. This was a new experience for him as he hadn't given himself the licence to think bigger and differently. By removing limits, Jonathan started to tap into his deepest aspirations. We suggested that he consider the following elements:

Self	Others	Business
Purpose – what is my big why?	*Relationships* – which type of people do I want to work with?	*Environment* – what represents the ideal conditions to work in?
Values – what are my deepest beliefs?		
Strengths – where do I get my energy from?	*Team* – how important is it to be around team players?	*Culture* – what are the type of norms I want to embrace?
Autonomy – how much do I want to direct my own life?		
Innovation – what role does creativity play and being prepared to do things differently?	*Influence* – what level of impact do I want to have?	*Sectors* – what industries excite me?
Learning – how do I want to be stretched and challenged?	*Leadership* – what does it mean to create followership?	*Companies* – who would I love to work with and why?
Mastery – what skills do I want to learn and improve?		
Success – what do I want to achieve?	*Management* – how do I want to invest in managing others?	*Structure* – what form of work do I want (e.g. employment, self-employment or entrepreneurial)?
Role – what type of roles inspire me?		
Reputation – what do I want to be known for?	*Development* – how much do I want to develop others?	
Recognition – how do I want to be remunerated?		
Contribution – what do I want to give back?		
Fulfilment – what do I enjoy?		
Wellbeing – how do I want to integrate health and vitality?		

Making time to 'pause' to understand yourself is a powerful investment. Slowing down to understand what fuels you helps you go faster and further. What we have noticed is that it is rare to come across people who have given sufficient thought to all these areas in a joined-up way. Some will have gone deep into certain aspects – for instance, focusing on the sector or role they would like to work in or the capability they need to succeed – and it can certainly be more straightforward to focus on these tangible aspects of work. However, the less tangible elements such as purpose, values, culture and contribution are harder to define and often get left out.

Jonathan jumped at the idea of developing a vision for his future. He could clearly see the logic of thinking ahead about what he wanted to help make his immediate path clearer in the here and now. To prepare him to think about his vision, we introduced him to a range of people so he could learn about their work stories. This enabled him to have more context to consider. He initiated conversations with highly supportive people in leadership, management and project roles covering multiple sectors. Jonathan then stepped back and started to dream. Gradually, he painted a picture that ignited his passion:

Self	Others	Business
Purpose – going beyond what he thought he was capable of	*Relationships* – building partnerships on high trust, respect and having fun together	*Culture* – being in an exciting, dynamic and authentic environment
Values – continuous learning, unlocking potential and working collaboratively	*Influence* – being known as an expert in his field and therefore able to have considerable impact	*Sectors* – operating in digital spaces that pioneer new services and have an entrepreneurial feel
Strengths – being relational, strategic thinking, problem solving and delivering on promises		
Autonomy – having the ability to direct his own life		

(*Continued*)

Self	Others	Business
Innovation – working in a high-paced, creative environment which pushes the boundaries of what is possible	*Leadership* – growing into a leadership role to get the best out of others	
Mastery – becoming a strategic thinker and delivering 'proof points' of great work done	*Management* – having the opportunity to build high-performing teams and develop others	
Success – hitting big goals that add real value		
Reputation – being known as a thought leader with subject matter expertise and being a great leader and manager		
Recognition – achieving the financial security to support his future family and lifestyle		
Contribution – leaving a meaningful mark by supporting those with less		
Fulfilment – understanding the world through global experiences and doing unique things		
Wellbeing – being fit, energetic with super optimism and high on life		

Jonathan was super-charged by the formation of his vision, which gave him a bigger picture to focus on. Out of this he was able to articulate a simple and memorable statement for his work vision: 'Make the impossible happen.' This newly formed vision energized Jonathan and provided a much deeper understanding of what work meant to him, thereby broadening his approach.

Jonathan's next step emerged out of a conversation with one of the leaders he interviewed who was so impressed by his passion, clarity and drive that she offered him work experience within the IT sector. We subsequently received a heartfelt note from Jonathan: 'I cannot thank you enough for your help in formulating my vision. I am taken aback to think where I was when we first spoke to where I am now.' The last message we received from him – on the completion of his first project, the installation of a new conference kit for the organiza-tion – was equally rewarding: 'The CEO said he's been waiting for a solution like this for years. He was really pleased, which made my day.'

Not figuring out your vision can have a profound impact, as Siân Evans, Director of Leadership and Colleague Experience at Simply-health, highlighted: 'One of the risks of not being clear about what you love to do is falling into work and finding yourself in a financial position where it becomes very difficult to make other choices. I have seen too many people endure what they do rather than having the courage to make tough decisions.' At the same time, she cautions against making any changes to meet your vision without the agree-ment of those closest to you:

If you have a family unit, agree with them that you have their support to go after your dream. Develop a transition plan to nudge you in the direction you want to go so that it is a manageable process. Keep checking in with yourself: am I still loving what I do and, if not, why not? I believe that once you make the decision to let go of the past, the future comes to you. You might take a diverse route to get to your ultimate passion but it's worth it.

The creation of vision activates possibility.

Henry Braithwaite, Founder of Lead Forensics, made a crucial point about lining things up clearly. Aligning your big-picture life plan with your mid- to long-term goals, current projects and today's tasks, he argues, is a very powerful act: 'I have been strongest at work when I have had clarity on everything. On the other hand I have found work toughest when it was more difficult to link all the pieces together.' For example, on achieving financial freedom he found it hard to justify work: why be in the office in an evening when he could be going out for a meal with friends? 'It became essential,' he told us, 'to reclarify the meaning I had for work and to reconcile how much I was going to trade off against my other goals.'

Susan was at a different point in her career. An outstanding lawyer with over 20 years in practice, Susan had worked tirelessly to reach partner level where she was now putting in 80-hour weeks. Trying to juggle being a mother, wife, daughter and friend and retain her sanity was wearing her out, and her exhaustion was compounded by a sense that she couldn't get off the hamster wheel she was running on. Susan was being asked by other partners to put herself forward for the managing partner election process for the firm and was in a dilemma as she reflected upon her options. We listened to her current reality as she painted a picture of what was happening. We summarized it as a state we call 'hyper-extension'. It was clear that if Susan continued at her current pace, she would at some point reach a threshold. We asked her about her vision for an ideal future. She took a deep breath and confessed that she had never stopped long enough to create one. We suggested that, before throwing her hat in for managing partner, it was the right time to dream up her future.

We met with Susan in a quiet café to remove her from the typical plush environments to which she was accustomed. We asked her to suspend her fierce logic and dream up her ideal future by standing ten years from now. Susan struggled with the concept and initially kept interrupting her visioning with apparent 'should and ought' scenarios arising from her current state, such as meeting client demands, the expectations of her associates and family needs. As these voices quietened, what emerged was a clear and compelling view of her deepest desires, aspirations and hopes. These included:

- **Justice** – Susan was originally drawn to law because of the opportunity to take a stand for what is right, fair and equitable. This voice had been quietened underneath the challenges of being a lawyer, but her vision brought it to the forefront of her awareness.
- **Partnership** – Susan had a passion for a partnership model, which again had become diminished by juggling multiple agendas.
- **Equality** – Susan was driven by creating equal opportunities and thrived on breaking down cultural norms and challenging expectations.
- **Innovation** – Susan loved coming up with new and different ways to solve problems.
- **Achievement** – Susan was driven by delivering results and value creation through meeting client needs.
- **Meaning** – Susan needed substance and to be involved in activities that enhanced things for the greater good.
- **Learning** – Susan had an insatiable appetite to learn, grow and unlock potential in herself and others.
- **Inspiration** – Susan wanted to be around people who fuelled her optimism and sense of possibility.
- **Memorability** – Susan recognized the importance of the present moment and wanted to create great memories.
- **Flourishing** – Susan was committed to integrating her work and life so that everyone got the best of her.

When Susan stepped back and reflected on her vision, she was genuinely inspired. However, her logic quickly kicked in and she started to question the reality of it and how she could go about putting it into action. We asked her to pause and draw breath. In *Helping People Change*, Boyatzis, Smith and Van Oosten (2019) describe the importance of activating a 'Positive Emotional Attractor' (PEA) which opens people up to possibilities and the excitement that comes with change. They cite research that shows that:

The energy and excitement around this Positive Emotional Attractor activate the parasympathetic nervous system, which sets into motion a set of physiological responses that put the person in a more relaxed and open state. Creative juices flow. New neural pathways form in the brain, thus paving the way for new learning and sustained behavioural change to occur.

Susan needed to become connected with her PEA so she could relax and think in different ways. The opposite of the PEA is the 'Negative Emotional Attractor' (NEA), which is activated when we are in survival mode. In this place any openness to new ideas and creativity is diminished. As Boyatzis, Smith and Van Oosten (2019) say: 'The NEA activates the sympathetic nervous system, and actually makes people physically less capable of learning, developing, or favourably changing behaviour.'

Fortunately, Susan had about 30 days before she needed to decide whether she was going to put herself forward for the managing partner election. We suggested that she take a few minutes each day to reflect upon her vision, and to start sharing some of it with those she trusted. Susan started with her husband. She described the amazing impact it had bringing him into her vision:

We hadn't had such an open and invigorating conversation in years. It was as if time rolled away, and we connected again with a raw energy and passion that had ignited our relationship at the beginning. My husband fully supported my vision and built upon it with some additional thoughts. We took pieces of it to our teenage children, who also resonated with concepts like justice, meaning and inspiration. I then shared elements with a couple of partners at the firm and was pleasantly surprised by their enthusiasm. It helped me to recognize that I was committed to the creation of my vision, and if becoming managing partner was the right thing to do it would be shown to me through the election process.

As part of the election process Susan needed to write her manifesto. She decided that the way to approach the task was through the lens of vision and to write her manifesto from her heart as well as from her head. She brought her guiding principles to life through a compelling narrative and then hit the campaign trail. Several weeks later, after engaging with each partner on an individual basis, Susan was tired but glowing. She had become genuinely inspired by sharing her vision, which tested her belief and commitment to it. When it came to the vote, Susan was relaxed about the outcome. She knew that whatever happened her work was never going to be the same. She had reset her context for doing what she loved and had a compelling vision pulling her forward. She could see that becoming managing partner would give her more leverage and opportunity to move the firm in the direction she wanted to go. However, if she didn't secure the role, it would provide extra fuel for her ability to bring the vision to fruition. Ultimately, she was successful in winning the vote, with the primary feedback being that partners could sense her passion for creating an inspiring future – it had become infectious.

What is the vision for doing the work you love and loving the work you do? Make the time to step back from your day-to-day task list and invest in the creation of your vision. Don't wait until you have all the jigsaw pieces of your vision in place. All great ideas start with an insight – a eureka moment – and can lead to creating a compelling vision of the future.

 **Lovenote**

Painting your vision of tomorrow ignites momentum today.

The power of intent

On awakening what is on your mind? What are the formative decisions you make/questions you have about the day? We have asked thousands of people over the years, and these are the usual responses we get:

- Check email/text/social media.
- Any overnight crises?

- What meetings have I got today?
- Where do I need to be?
- How's the weather?
- What am I going to wear?
- Hit snooze … again!
- Tea or coffee?
- Walk the dog.

Visionary? No.
Inspiring? No.
Predictable? Yes!

It's a 'to do' list based on the question 'What have I got to do today?' and goes on to shape your day. But there are various types of questions you can ask that will help you think differently and shape your work in a conscious way:

What do I appreciate today?

What am I looking forward to?

What difference can I make today?

What's possible today?

How do I want to be today?

Research supports our point here. Asking yourself thought-provoking questions awakens your Positive Emotional Attractor (PEA), which activates the parts of your brain that trigger the hormones – the parasympathetic nervous system (PNS) – associated with emotions such as awe, joy, gratitude and curiosity. On the other hand, asking the wrong questions arouses your Negative Emotional Attractor (NEA), which activates different brain networks and triggers hormones that activate your sympathetic nervous system (SNS), putting you in survival mode where your creativity and openness to new ideas are limited (Boyatzis, Smith and Van Oosten, 2019).

It's helpful to understand how our brains have the ability to adapt (known as neuroplasticity), as explained by neuropsychologist Celeste Campbell:

[Neuroplasticity] refers to the physiological changes in the brain that happen as the result of our interactions with our environment. From the time the brain begins to develop in utero until the day we die, the connections among the cells in our brains reorganize in response to our changing needs. This dynamic process allows us to learn from and adapt to different experiences. (Campbell, 2009)

Building on the notion of the brain's neuroplasticity is the insight that we can develop the connections in our brains and learn to be inspired due to the linkage between neuroplasticity and a growth mindset. Psychologist Courtney E. Ackerman explains the connection in more detail:

The concepts mirror each other; a growth mindset is a mindset that one's innate skills, talents, and abilities can be developed and/or improved with determination, while neuroplasticity refers to the brain's ability to adapt and develop beyond the usual developmental period of childhood. A person with a growth mindset believes that he or she can get smarter, better, or more skilled at something through sustained effort – which is exactly what neuroplasticity tells us. You might say that a growth mindset is simply accepting the idea of neuroplasticity on a broad level. (Ackerman, 2021)

Inspiration is not for a chosen few. Anyone can become more inspired by asking the right questions and developing the right mindset, which starts with the power of intention.

Characteristics of being intentional include:

- slow and logical decision making
- being thoughtful and selective
- conscious and deliberate actions.

You know that you are being intentional when:

- **Your work is purposeful.** You are clear about why you are doing what you are doing and your intrinsic motivation. You are driven by what is meaningful.
- **You make time for conscious thinking.** You slow down and create space for reflection. You enjoy taking time to think.
- **You prioritize what matters most.** You focus on what is most important and can let go of the rest. You resist the temptation to be busy for the sake of being busy.
- **You are fully present.** You have heightened awareness about what is happening and operate in the moment.
- **You are doing the work you want.** You have the experience of flow and being in the right place at the right time.

The opposite of intentionality is autopilot. This is when we make unconscious, automatic decisions to help with certain routine tasks. It is an evolutionary mechanism that has developed to stop our brains from overloading. Yet, today, making choices on autopilot has seeped into more areas of our life and work, taking us away from what we truly want. When we live on autopilot, it feels like someone else is driving, not us. Characteristics of operating on autopilot include:

- quick and impulsive decision making
- being biased and habitual
- unconscious and automatic actions.

You know that you are working on autopilot when:

- **Your work is predictable.** Your schedule is full of repetitive activities, and you follow your plan without thinking. There is no room for spontaneity or changing the routine.
- **Your work primarily pleases others.** You let other people's expectations define your choices. You fail to pay attention to what you need.
- **You are always on.** You rarely pause to reflect on how you are feeling at work or what you are doing. You are busy, distracted or hyperactive.
- **You are not present.** You can't remember what you accomplished throughout the day. You feel guilty that you haven't done what you set out to achieve.
- **You believe you are missing out.** You know that you can have more fulfilment in what you do, but you don't know how to make it happen.

Being on autopilot has its benefits for mundane activities, such as driving or food shopping. However, it is an inhibitor when you want to be intentional and need to resolve an issue or fuel your fire in conscious ways.

> Inspiration starts with intention.

Probably the most powerful technology to help us be intentional, overcome autopilot, develop a growth mindset and strengthen our Positive Emotional Attractor is mindfulness. In its simplest form, mindfulness is the ability to pay attention. It is not just the practice of meditation. It is a way of basing yourself on a higher state of awareness that enables you to quieten your mind and enhance your decision making. It allows you to develop a peaceful mind and have greater awareness about the here and now.

Professor Mark Williams, former director of the Oxford Mind-fulness Centre, says that mindfulness means knowing directly what is going on inside and outside ourselves, moment by moment. 'It's easy,' he says, 'to stop noticing the world around us. It's also easy to lose touch with the way our bodies are feeling and to end up living "in our heads" – caught up in our thoughts without stopping to notice how those thoughts are driving our emotions and behaviour.' He argues that an important part of mindfulness is reconnecting with our bodies and the sensations they experience: 'This means waking up to the sights, sounds, smells and tastes of the present moment. That might be something as simple as the feel of a banister as we walk upstairs.' Another key part of mindfulness is to be aware of our thoughts and feelings as they occur moment to moment: 'It's about allowing ourselves to see the present moment clearly. When we do that, it can positively change the way we see ourselves and our lives.'

Sara Lazar, a neuroscientist at Massachusetts General Hospital and Harvard Medical School, was one of the first scientists to take the anecdotal claims about the benefits of meditation and mindfulness and test them in brain scans. What she found surprised her: meditating can, quite literally, change your brain. She and her team found that people who have meditated for a long time have an increased amount of grey matter in the insula and sensory regions, the auditory and sensory cortex. This, she argues, makes perfect sense: 'When you're mindful, you're paying attention to your breathing, to sounds, to the present moment experience, and shutting cognition down. It stands to reason your senses would be enhanced. We also found they had more grey matter in the frontal cortex, which is associated with working memory and executive decision making.' In a study of the brains of two groups of subjects, one of which had learned mindfulness for stress reduction, the other which had not, she found that the first group had thickening in four regions:

1 the **posterior cingulate** – which is involved in mind wandering and self-relevance
2 the **left hippocampus** – which assists in learning, cognition, memory and emotional regulation
3 the **temporal–parietal junction** (TPJ) – which is associated with perspective taking, empathy and compassion

4 the **pons** – where a lot of regulatory neurotransmitters are
   produced.

Lazar and her team also found that the amygdala – the 'fight or
flight' part of the brain – which is important for anxiety, fear and
stress in general – got smaller in the group that went through the
mindfulness-based stress-reduction programme.

We find that people are often put off by the idea of mindfulness,
believing they will need to schedule long periods of time to practise
things like meditation and yoga. However, research shows that simply
committing to 10 minutes of mindfulness training each day makes a
considerable difference. This training can be as simple as sitting upright
in a chair, placing your attention on your breathing and simply observing it. When you find yourself distracted by a sound or sensation, bring
your attention back to your breath. Notice your inhale and exhale.
Don't try to control your breathing. Be aware of the sensation of each
breath. Don't try to control your thinking. Be aware of any thoughts
coming and going from your mind and bring your attention back to
your breathing. Don't try to control your feelings. Be aware of any
feelings that surface and bring your focus back to your breathing. At
the end of 10 minutes take a few deeper breaths, stretch and you're
ready to go.

There are other actions you can take to develop mindfulness
including:

- **Avoiding logging on to email and social media first
  thing in the morning.** These can create distractions and
  take you away from the opportunity to be reflective,
  thoughtful, focused and creative.
- **Stopping multi-tasking helps you to be more mindful
  during a day.** When we try to do too many things at once,
  it causes us to be reactive and reduces our awareness.
- **Scheduling time to check in with yourself each week
  to review your levels of mindfulness.** You can ask
  yourself: 'On a scale of 1–10 (10 representing heightened
  mindfulness), how mindful was I this week?'; 'How present

have I been?'; 'How conscious of my choices and actions?';
'How peaceful have I been?'; 'How consistent have I been
with my thinking, communication and actions?'

Ultimately, mindfulness is having heightened awareness about
yourself, others and the context around you. It gives you an ability
to observe what's going on, rather than be unconsciously driven
by it. It also supports a mindset that nurtures curiosity, creativity and calm that can stimulate some of your best thinking. Here
are some well-known people who meditate, which nourishes their
mindfulness:

- **Bill Gates:** 'I now see that meditation is simply exercise for
  the mind, similar to the way we exercise our muscles when
  we play sports. For me, it has nothing to do with faith or
  mysticism. It's about taking a few minutes out of my day,
  learning how to pay attention to the thoughts in my head,
  and gaining a little bit of distance from them.'
- **Katy Perry:** 'It's changed my life; it's changed how I think
  about things. I meditate before I write a song, before I
  perform. I feel my brain open up and I feel my most sharp.'
- **Jerry Seinfeld:** 'When I think about the things I love more
  than money, more than love, more than just about anything,
  I love energy. I love it and I pursue it, I want it, and I
  want more of it. And I think this is the reason by the way
  why I'm so enthusiastic about Transcendental Meditation.
  Physical and mental energy to me are the greatest riches of
  human life. And Transcendental Meditation is like this free
  account of an endless amount of it.'

We have been practising mindfulness for over 30 years and yet still
consider ourselves novices. It is a never-ending journey to expand
awareness, pay attention and be present, yet worth every moment.
Make the shift from autopilot to being mindful about your intention
to thrive at work.

> **♥ Lovenote**
>
> When we work on autopilot, it's as if an inanimate machine
> is driving, not us. Shifting to an intentional mode puts us
> in charge of the direction we want to go and enables us to
> respond to what happens in a fully human way.

Conversations that matter

One of the most important ways to develop and sustain the fuel
for inspiration is through conversation. We forget that conversation
is a form of work and that the quality of our conversations determines the quality of our work. As Alan Webber, erstwhile editor of
the *Harvard Business Review*, says 'The most important work in the
new economy is creating conversations' (Webber, 1993).

It's vital to engage in bigger conversations that inspire us and make
us want to develop and change for the better. The trouble is that
many of us are too busy to prioritize meaningful conversations as we
get consumed by task. We have identified nine essential ingredients
for having big conversations:

1 Be intentional	Be clear about the primary intent that lies behind your conversations – for instance, to trust, to connect or to understand. The brain has mirror neurons which codify the actions of other people and also our own actions. They are essential brain cells for social interaction and picking up on other people's intentions and emotions.
2 Be present	If you're not able to pay attention and give your time and energy to a conversation, wait until you can. It's better to commit to shorter and more frequent conversations when you can actually be there rather than get distracted and break connection.

(Continued)

3 Be humble	Probably one of the most damaging traits to demonstrate in conversation is arrogance, particularly in the form of thinking you are 'right'. This can originate from internal insecurities or adopting a 'fixed' mindset, and becomes an immediate blocker to the conditions required for a free-flowing conversation. When you are in the presence of humility, it creates an environment of safety and non-judgement where people can be without defensiveness and display compassion.
4 Be open	Bias is part of being human. However, part of a meaningful conversation is to be able to suspend judgement so that you can actively participate. Challenge yourself to keep an open mind, and when you feel your hot buttons getting pushed, use it as a lever to rise above your conditioned responses.
5 Be empathetic	One of our deepest human needs is to be understood. Empathy is the ability to truly put yourself in the shoes of others and seek to understand their perspective, their reality, their experience, their version of truth. It's a difficult muscle to exercise as we are tempted to slip back into trying to meet our needs, but giving to others through empathy is one of the best investments you can make.
6 Be curious	Probably the most important ingredient to provoke great conversations is to bring intense curiosity. The definition of curiosity in the *Oxford English Dictionary* is 'a strong desire to know or learn something'. Have you experienced an 'aha!' moment, or eureka moment, that gives you the momentum to make progress? This type of insight is activated by curiosity.
7 Be adaptable	In any conversation it's vital to flex, adopt a change mindset and be agile in your approach. There is no one fixed point in a conversation but multiple data points which, if embraced, can enrich the topic in hand.

8 Be optimistic	If you engaged in a conversation about vision it is important to help someone feel hopeful about the future. In *Helping People Change*, Boyatzis, Smith and Van Oosten reference an fMRI study that shows that spending 30 minutes in a conversation about a person's vision or dream activates regions of the brain associated with imagining new things and more parasympathetic nervous system activity. Optimism is an ability – allowing you to see the potential of what's coming and to focus on the next steps to move things forward.
9 Be appreciative	Approaching a conversation through the lens of appreciative inquiry means that you build upon strengths, focus on what's working and acknowledge others' contributions.

Our first live event working with a team during the COVID-19 crisis was with an operational leadership team within the transportation sector. It was September 2020, and the team hadn't been together in person for nearly seven months. During that period they had been consumed by task, initially in crisis management mode and, more latterly, with adjusting to an unpredictable reality focused on people, financial and operational requirements.

We started by providing an opportunity to 'check in', listening to what was on people's minds and how they had fared over the last few months. Ninety minutes later the team had reconnected and blown away the cobwebs of endless hours on Microsoft Teams. The conversation covered topics such as coping with home schooling, thriving on disruption, clarifying new roles, making big operational changes, and managing physical and mental health. Although the team were itching to get on with the day's agenda, we reminded them that conversation is a form of work and that it was essential for them to reconnect before jumping into more action.

Our next conversation was about their purpose as a team. Given the fact that new members had joined, and the breadth of the team had expanded, it was important for them to discuss why they existed and what their contribution was beyond the delivery of tangible metrics. This opened up a meaningful conversation which led to an exploration about a range of factors which people felt strongly about – including improving people's lives by enabling them to get to work, seeing family and keeping the economy going.

We then entered into one-to-one feedback conversations where everyone had the chance to share what they appreciated about working with one another and the support they needed from each team member to help them succeed. This unlocked deeper levels of empathy and understanding, strengthening their collective foundation of trust and getting to know one another in new ways.

The final conversation was about how they could apply their learnings from day one back in the business. They agreed a series of important areas to cover, including managing people, simplifying processes, improving meetings and preparing for a further COVID-19 wave. Four big conversations were held in one day which had an exponential impact on their work going forward. In the absence of conversation, the team would simply not have had the opportunity to clarify and align on major issues, thus saving them precious time and resource going forward.

> Great conversations lead to great work.

How do you prioritize conversation to improve the quality of your work and help others along the way? In our multimedia world, conversations take on many different forms. It's amazing to think that email and text now seem almost passé with the advent of e-chat applications which allow for seamless communications between team members and the sharing of ideas, messages, documents and videos. These are brilliant for increasing efficiencies and navigating an increasingly virtual workplace; however, they should not offer a full replacement of conversation in person.

In 2019 the ADP Research Institute (ADPRI) surveyed over 19,000 workers across the globe to measure their levels of engagement and identify what conditions at work are most likely to attract and keep workers. They found that teams and trust in team leaders are the most important influences on employee engagement. In his book *Nine Lies about Work* (co-authored with Ashley Goodall), one of the ADPRI lead researchers, Marcus Buckingham, draws upon the findings and makes a highly significant observation:

> If you study the best team leaders you'll discover that many of them share a frequent sense-making ritual … it's called a check-in. In simple terms it's a frequent one-on-one conversation about near-term future work between a team leader and a team member. How frequent? Every week during which they ask two simple questions: What are your priorities this week? How can I help? (Buckingham and Goodall, 2019)

The quality of conversations you have at work determines the quality of your work. However, having great conversations doesn't mean that they are simply nice and fluffy. Often, the most rewarding conversations we have at work are the toughest.

Catherine is an amazingly creative designer. In one of our coaching conversations she described how she was drained and troubled by a particular relationship. One of her team members was not performing in role and it was putting her function at risk. There were mitigating circumstances. The impact of COVID-19 meant that the team member was having to deal with limited resource, she was home-schooling two young children and was the primary earner in the family. Catherine is big-hearted and cares passionately about her people. However, this team member had been complaining to her for over six months, she was failing to bring solutions and Catherine was at breaking point. We asked her whether she'd had a direct conversation with the team member to resolve the issue. Catherine was concerned that the person involved would react badly, blame the lack of resource, get angry and it would backfire on Catherine.

We coached Catherine on how to use an effective tool for having difficult conversations – Every Fish Needs Batter and Chips:

- **E is for Explanation** – presenting the facts.
- **F is for Feelings** – sharing the emotional impact.
- **N is for Needs** – clarifying what needs to happen to resolve the issue.
- **B is for Benefits** – stating what's in it for both parties to make progress.
- **C is for Consequences** – stating what will happen if things are not resolved. (Don't, however, share the consequences unless you will definitely act on them.)

Catherine wrote out what she wanted to communicate using the tool, and this enabled her to have a direct and constructive conversation with the team member. Together, they came up with new solutions for managing the limited resource and agreed that the team member would re-engage with a positive approach to delivering creative solutions, which is what she loved in her work.

Having open and direct conversations is a skill. Some cultures advocate 'radical transparency' for communicating. In our experience most people are not ready for such levels of exposure. We spend a lot of our time helping individuals and teams learn how to start to converse in constructive ways, which, once developed, provide a foundation for doing great work.

Make big conversations part of the way you work. Find people with whom you resonate, with whom you can have conversations that inspire you, and who make you want to develop, change and grow. Try, for example, talking to someone about your vision. As Boyatzis, Smith and Van Oosten say in *Helping People Change*: 'We know from sports psychology research, meditation and biofeedback that we can engage emotional commitment if we can give life to our dreams. A compelling vision transforms purpose into action, makes order out of chaos, instils confidence and drives us to fulfil a desired future' (Boyatzis, Smith and Van Oosten, 2019). Talk about your dreams so that you are fuelled, energized and committed to doing the work you love, because the ability to have meaningful and inspiring conversations is one of the most powerful forms of work.

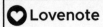 **Lovenote**

Bigger and better conversations lead to stronger and smarter work.

At the heart of it

If you want to love what you do,
you need to do what inspires you.

If you want to be inspired, dream;
have the courage to think bigger.

This is a choice.

If you want to make this happen,
link inspiration to intention.

If you want to build momentum,
ignite the energy and enthusiasm of others.

**Small sparks multiplied by a big vision
leads to magical results.**

3
Unlock your code

Crucibles and the compass

Roger Hunt had a calm presence and a quiet way of interacting. When he spoke, people listened – and with reason. On 26 November 2008, India came under a series of horrific terrorist attacks which killed more than 150 people and injured hundreds more. Roger was working for the Royal Bank of Scotland at the time and was staying at the Oberoi Trident Hotel in Mumbai where he found himself caught up in a siege. Trapped in his hotel room, defenceless against the suicidal terrorists who were killing people in cold blood, Roger was forced to rely on his instinct. His account of his terrifying ordeal was at once poignant and gripping – a raw, honest narration of how an ordinary man was thrown into the path of danger and pushed to the limit in his struggle for survival. Naturally, it was a life-changing experience.

We were fortunate to have Roger attend one of our leadership development programmes several years after his ordeal. As part of the learning process we invited participants to identify turning points, or 'crucible moments', from their lives. We asked them to recognize the impact of those events and to define how they informed their values. Roger's story has been one of the most significant we have heard over the years. Reflecting on how this experience had affected him, he commented:

> This experience has given me a different perspective. I will never take comfort and an easy existence for granted; I now fully appreciate the importance of family, friends and loyal work colleagues. In the West, it's all too easy to put out of our minds the gulf between rich and poor, how the world of the 'haves' is so starkly paralleled by that of the 'have-nots'.

The impact of being caught up in the attack caused Roger to reflect on what was most important for him and how he wanted to work and live. It brought him closer to his core values of people and the sacredness of life. From a work perspective he chose to leave the world of banking to join the Scottish Prison Service, where he was HR Manager for two prisons before moving to Aberdeen Airport as Chief Human Resources and Development Director. He has also been regularly involved in activities supporting counter-terrorism, contributing to hostage work alongside the likes of Terry Waite. He went on to write a compelling book about his experience in India, *Be Silent or Be Killed* (2011).

Your values come from learned experience, usually times of adversity. A crucible is a container in which metals are subjected to extremely high temperatures, and a 'crucible moment' is a situation where an individual is severely tested and undergoes a transformation as a result. Values reflect what is important to you and become a shorthand way of describing your motivations. Together with your beliefs, they are the causal factors that drive your decision making. To discover your values, you need to trace the critical events from your life, the lessons you learned and the conclusions you formed. Let's look at some examples.

At the age of 13 Rupal was sent to a boarding school run by nuns in the foothills of the Himalayas by her well-meaning parents. She found it oppressive and dictatorial, and it suffocated her spirit. On holidays, she would discuss it with her parents, but they refused to consider a change. At the age of 15, Rupal took the bold decision to run away from her school to the city. Her parents disowned her and told her not to return home. She managed to find odd jobs and continued her education. Aged 18, she applied for university and just failed to secure a place. Undeterred, she stepped up her learning and the following year passed the entrance exams. These times of adversity cemented her values of freedom, independence and perseverance.

John's father was a brilliant businessman. He had grown the family company into a successful enterprise. He was John's hero. However, they had very little time together due to the demands of the business. When John was 15, his father died. John was devastated. He came out in a rash and developed chronic eczema. This caused him to hide away and not want to be seen. John went on a wayward path, feeling alone and fearing that he would never live up to his father's expectations. Eventually, he formed a strong bond with a mentor who was able to help John come to terms with his loss and pick up the pieces of his life. John's values of resilience, together with his determination to give back and nurture strong relationships, have formed the basis of a rewarding career alongside the creation of his own loving family.

Gina is an award-winning lawyer who blends an insatiable work ethic with a passion for fairness, inclusion and the provision of equal opportunities for minorities. Originating from Asia, Gina grew up in a strict environment that cemented her work discipline alongside an awareness of the oppression faced by many women. She was repeatedly told that she would not have the chance to further her education and fulfil her potential. She had to rally against this cultural blueprint, and this strengthened her resolve to prove her oppressors wrong. Her determination resulted in Gina flying through her education with the highest marks, and slowly she began to quieten her doubters. Now as General Counsel for a FTSE 100 company and founder of a charity for women who have suffered domestic abuse in her hometown, Gina is a role model for many.

Values form the core beliefs which become part of your code.

What are the crucible moments that have influenced you? What have you learned? What are your values which form the blueprint for how you work and live? To do the work you love, it's essential to have clarity about your values as they shape your mindset, inform your decision making and drive your actions. Some of your values will fully support doing the work you love. On the other hand, you may be driven by certain values that act as an unconscious barrier to doing what you love. Either way, having heightened awareness about your values and how they impact you moves you in the direction you want to go, as well as helping others understand you.

There are four steps to defining your values in a process known as a lifeline:

1 Event	2 Impact	3 Learning	4 Value
Chronologically mark the key experiences and turning points that have shaped your life so far. These are sometimes called 'crucible' moments and are usually associated with adversity, setbacks and failures, e.g. family, education, relational, bereavement, life and career	Against each event note the impact that it had on you, e.g. sense of loss, betrayal, injustice, failure, frustration, achievement	Reflect upon the learning you gained, and conclusion formed from the experience, e.g. setbacks make you resilient, injustice can motivate, loss helps you appreciate life, achievement drives ambition	Identify the specific value linked to the learning, e.g. honesty, optimism, fairness, respect, safety, opportunity

Use this lifeline framework to help you define your values. Here is an example:

1 Event	2 Impact	3 Learning	4 Value
Failing school exams	Sense of injustice and formation of an internalized belief of being 'less than' and 'not good enough'	Importance of challenging the system and finding alternative ways to unlock potential	Independence

Divorce of parents	Feeling betrayed, let down and disappointed; low trust of others	Not taking anything for granted; challenging the status quo	Resilience
Loss of a major work transaction	Sense of helplessness at not being able to turn things around and make it happen	Importance of serendipity, timing and being in the right place at the right time	Trust
Working hard to deliver on a key project	Driven by work ethic, challenging self and overcoming roadblocks	Significance of playing to strengths and drawing energy from stretching goals	Success

Here are a few pointers to get the most out of this exercise:

- You might find that you have numerous events. There are no limits. Write them all down. Explore patterns. Identify the links between the impact, learning and your core values.
- You might be clear about your values, but not what has shaped them. If so, write down your values and then go back and reflect on where they have come from.

Most events tend to be connected with adversity as we often learn and grow from our most challenging experiences. However, if you believe you've led a charmed life, then count your blessings and continue to identify the events that have had the biggest impact on you and how they have defined what's most important.

Once you have completed a first draft, find a trusted partner to share your lifeline with. Talking these experiences through with another person can be a valuable part of the process, as articulating it out loud helps develop your insight. Your 'thinking partner' can support and challenge you to clarify your thoughts.

Keith Barr, CEO of IHG, clearly articulates the importance of values:

Make sure your work fits with who you are. Ask yourself: Does my work align with my values and who I am? For instance, I am hard-wired to care. During COVID-19 my commitment was to make sure that we could keep as many people employed for as long as possible based on what we could afford to do. I also held monthly calls with 6,000 colleagues which were live and unscripted and faced into the tough questions to make sure people felt cared for … Make sure you work for a company whose culture and values make you feel good when you go home at night, even when times are tough.

Laura Miller, Executive Vice President and Chief Information Officer at Macy's, reinforces this approach by describing how values can be a deal-breaker at work:

Everyone needs to live within their own values. If you get out of bed and you are questioning decisions being made at work that don't relate to your values, you need to think hard about where you want to be. I have values like honesty and sticking to your word which when absent causes me to shut down. I then try to remove myself from the situation and often will look for somewhere else to go.

John Holland-Kaye, CEO at Heathrow, puts it this way:

I have got the most out of work where my values have been aligned with the company I'm working with. On the other hand, I have found the most stressful times at work have occurred when my values were challenged by the organization. I appreciate that when you're working in a company it's harder to align personal and organizational values because you don't set the agenda, but it's often a deal-breaker if they are too at odds. One of the priorities I have always set while working on executive committees and now as a CEO is to utilize the opportunity to shape the company values in order to create strong alignment with the people I work with, which makes work far more enjoyable. You can also get a sense of real achievement in terms of what matters beyond financial reward.

Values are not soft and fluffy. They are the hard stuff in work which often determines who works where and what gets done. Once you have identified them, the challenge is to live them on a consistent basis. The way to live your values is to evidence what they mean in action. The following table shows an example of how to make your values tangible by identifying what it would look like at work if you were living them on a consistent basis:

Value	Evidence	Actions
Honesty	Speaking from the heart Having voice without fear of negative consequences Being able to go direct to people and sharing a point of view	Agree expectations with line manager about the licence to be honest Set expectations with team members about what honesty looks like as a team Request feedback from stakeholders to accurately assess the impact of honesty
Trust	Assuming good intent Displaying humility and vulnerability Taking accountability for personal actions	Take regular 'pulse checks' with team members to measure trust levels Create opportunity for personal storytelling to build emotional connection in relationships Give feedback when actions don't match intent
Learning	Demonstrating a growth mindset Turning 'problems' into development opportunities Seeking ways to stretch and be challenged	Have an authentic and active personal development plan Invest time in coaching and mentoring conversations Attend learning events like conferences and workshops to explore new ideas and practices

Once you have defined what it will look like to live your values at work, here are some approaches to embed them.

Values partner

Find someone with whom you can develop a supportive and challenging relationship to be your values conscience. This is also sometimes called an 'accountability partnership'. Work together to identify your evidence and actions and give them permission to hold you accountable to your word.

Sarah and Daniel formed a values partnership on the back of one of our leadership development programmes. Sarah was in a difficult position at work, as her line manager rubbed up against her values set. Her line manager showed low trust, micromanaged and was highly directive in his style. These behaviours contrasted with Sarah's value of autonomy, evidenced through giving people time and space to think, operate and learn from their mistakes.

Sarah and Daniel met at a time when Sarah was looking for other roles and was ready to quit against her preferred option of staying within the company. They made an agreement that each time Sarah felt disturbed by her manager's behaviour, Sarah would text Daniel with the code word TRIGGER before she reacted. This would buy her some breathing space and stop her from over-reacting in the moment. Daniel would be able to step in, sometimes with a question to provoke her thinking or simply a listening ear to let her download. Sarah never came to agree with her line manager's approach, but over time she was able to change the way she responded, which lessened the impact. This strengthened her sense of autonomy as she wasn't jumping to her manager's directive. Eventually, the manager left, as his approach didn't fit with the wider company's values. Sarah gained a promotion and has since gone from strength to strength.

It is inevitable that your values will be tested over time, so forming a values partnership can become a rich source of strength.

Values journal

A life worth living is a life worth recording. A values journal is a helpful tool to use. This is a space for you to record your intent, learnings, reflections, commitments, insights and feelings associated with living your values at work. We believe it's important to not be overly prescriptive about how to use your journal; however, making time to reflect is an essential requirement for a healthy work experience. On awakening, reach for your values journal and write down your intent for the day. For instance, if one of your values is 'integrity', writing down one way you will 'do the right thing' in the coming day reinforces your intent. It's a space where you can look at what it means to live your values and the impact of doing so.

Listen to yourself. Don't judge or evaluate what you write. Quieten the 'inner critic' so that you give rise to the voice within. For those who like more structure, we recommend writing for three minutes uninterrupted. This clears your mind and gives you enough time to deepen your thinking. So often we run at such a pace in a day that we fail to slow down long enough to truly consider what is going on. A values journal will enable you to raise your awareness and increase your sensory acuity about what works, what doesn't work and what you want to do differently to strengthen your values.

Values cards

It can be an insightful exercise to create your own pack of values cards. Get hold of a stack of index cards and on each one write down a value and/or a value statement. It could look like the following:

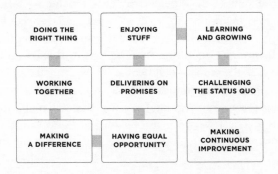

Keep the cards handy. If you are struggling with a decision or preparing for a difficult conversation, evaluating your options can be an effective way of strengthening your resilience, and/or coming up with a solution. If you work in an office with a desk, making them visible might lead to some interesting conversations. If you lead a team, it can be a way of helping people understand you through a values lens by sharing what you believe in.

Team values

We were asked to coach the retail leadership team in an organization. After experiencing considerable change over a two-year period with different leaders in role, they had built up some severe baggage that was weighing them down. Relations were strained. Trust was low. Conflict was high. People were working in silos and failing to share what they were working on, which was causing duplication and slowing progress. The new leader was values-based and wanted to rebuild the team, starting with shared values. We met with each team member to canvass views about the current state of the team and future aspirations. It became clear that many of the issues were caused by a lack of alignment about what people valued. This was demonstrated by their behaviours at work.

When we brought the team together for an offsite, our starting point was to look at values. We recognized that unless there was common ground about what the team believed, everything else would be seen as lip service. We asked each team member to write down their top three personal values. We heard from everyone and then grouped the values into different categories including relationships (trust, respect, inclusion), integrity (fairness, safety, accountability), success (achievement, performance, results) and fulfilment (happiness, freedom, learning). One of the challenges of working with values in an organizational context is that people can become frustrated by the lack of tangible action demonstrating the espoused values. As a result, we advise teams to only sign up for values that will help move them forward in practical ways. We also encourage teams to use everyday language that pinpoints emotion. In this instance, after constructive debate, the retail leadership team arrived at the following values to help them be aligned:

- Assume good intent.
- Go direct.
- Let go.
- Get stuff done.

There was an energy about these values that captured their imagination. They were simple and meaningful and addressed some of the core issues about lack of trust, going behind people's backs, holding on to the past and failing to deliver results. The leader was determined to make them a way of working rather than just a set of words. At each team meeting, she set aside time at the start of the agenda to highlight a particular value, for instance 'Go direct'. To encourage shared learning, she would ask for a couple of examples where team members had put this into practice, including what they had done and how they had done it. She also then asked for a couple of examples where people were struggling with living this value. This had a secondary benefit of supporting psychological safety within the team, creating an environment where people felt able to speak up and share without the fear of negative consequences.

If you're a team leader, engage your team with the idea of defining shared values. If you're part of a team and think it would be a good idea to explore this area, suggest it to the rest of the team and see what reaction it provokes. It can work with all kinds of teams. For instance, we know a number of non-exec boards which have agreed 'Board Team Values' to help with more efficient and effective ways of working. Having clear team values provides an aligned way of working leading to better results.

Company values

We've heard it all before ... those bland, meaningless corporate values paraded in documents and at meetings or even flashed over posters and signage. Don't do it. You are not going to create an environment where people love their work based on platitudes. Company values should be the intent behind an organizational culture; in other words, they show 'the way we do things around here'. However, when they are not authentically lived, it can bring companies to their knees. They need to be in people's heads and hearts, not just written on walls and mugs.

At its peak, Enron was an energy, commodities and services company employing nearly 22,000 people. Based in Houston, Texas, Enron was one of the largest energy companies in the world and had been named 'America's most innovative company' for six consecutive years by *Fortune* magazine. In its annual report to shareholders (Enron, Annual Report, 2000: 29), Enron listed its core values as:

- **Communication** – we have an obligation to communicate.
- **Respect** – we treat others as we would like to be treated.
- **Integrity** – we work with customers and prospects openly, honestly and sincerely.
- **Excellence** – we are satisfied with nothing less than the very best in everything we do.

When the Enron scandal hit in 2001, a series of events was unleashed that resulted in the bankruptcy of the company, which held more than $60 billion in assets, as well as the dissolution of Arthur Andersen LLP which had been one of the largest auditing and accounting companies in the world. The global exposure of the reality of the way the organization worked became, in effect, a public mockery of its stated 'values'. The actions of leadership were revealed to have established a culture of greed and pride. The behaviours of those inside the organization showed clearly that this was not a culture that lived the values it espoused.

We have seen similar instances closer to home. For example, we were introduced to a fast-and-furious digital start-up where employees had an average tenure of 18 months. The company bled people dry – even seriously smart performers quickly suffered burnout. The CEO simply didn't care. Although he talked about the values being 'at the core of everything we do, guiding how we work and make decisions', the reality was that if someone didn't keep up, he trashed them publicly and got them out. He was known as a 'bully', and his leadership style cast a shadow of fear. Unsurprisingly, we had one meeting to discuss the company culture, shared our point of view and were never invited back.

On another occasion we were invited to meet an organization which claimed to be a great place to work, put people first, and celebrate diversity and inclusion. In our initial diagnostic, we discovered an environment where people were afraid of 'rocking the boat' in case they lost their jobs, where sizable amounts of money were spent on creating glossy PowerPoint decks to make everything 'look good', and where 'glass ceilings' prevented some from career progression. These findings were shared with the main stakeholders, together with some recommendations for what needed to happen next. The organization's discomfort with our candid findings led to a decision not to move forward with the project.

We know of many infinitely more positive examples, however. We have previously referred to working with edyn, the inspiring hospitality company that expresses its values as 'The courage to question, to evolve, to be human'. In our interview with its CEO, Stephen McCall, he spoke about two of the core values that have been incorporated into the fabric of the company – individuality and freedom. 'At edyn we celebrate the individual, which means recognizing personal values and preferences at work.' One way in which this was put into practice was the removal of the dress code, as 'putting on a persona didn't fit with who we are as a company'. 'Having an environment where people have to behave in careful, odd and guarded ways makes work extremely difficult. In our business of soulful hospitality it's about being in touch with what you love and expressing it.'

Likewise, the company value of freedom is expressed through no longer having core working hours: 'One of the lessons with COVID-19 is that it has reinforced our concept of freedom. Today I am sitting in the garden and calling it work. The weird imposition of a morning commute, doing eight hours of work and arriving home exhausted is a tragedy.' McCall pointed out that there was considerable resistance to removing the dress code and work hours, along with creating flatter structures and having ambiguous decision making, but he persisted: 'In order to have an authentic business we needed to advocate an authentic culture. People are still questioning it, which is healthy, but at some point they will need to embrace it, or it simply won't be the right environment.'

Who do you want to work with and why? We find that more and more people make decisions about who they work with based on values and culture, over more traditional factors like pay and status. In the June 2020 *Harvard Business Review* issue entitled 'Emerging from the crisis', there is an insightful 'roundtable' article by Adi Ignatius, 'What is the next normal going to look like?' Geoff Martha, CEO of Medtronic has noted that companies are being watched in terms of how they treat staff, customers, clients and investors. A younger generation of employees will make decisions on who they work for in part as a result of these observations.

Companies today need to check their 'say/do' ratio. When there is trust in what you say, there will be belief in what you will do. People are fed up with empty rhetoric and meaningless words. Adopt a 'say/do' ratio of one to one. If a company says it 'cares about people', it needs to evidence this in a tangible way – for instance, by taking regular 'pulse checks' with employees to understand the emotional climate and address any issues. During the COVID-19 crisis we partnered with an organization which stepped up its investment in people. We had the opportunity to work closely with two different leadership teams on a weekly basis. By June 2020 people were close to burnout having adopted a relentless working schedule. When we explored the topic, what emerged was that one of the causal factors was the absence of a clear organizational decision-making framework and that this had resulted in duplicated work, constant checking and going around in circles. We requested some volunteers to come up with recommendations to share with the executive committee. By mid-July a new decision-making framework was implemented into the business focused on making lives easier (a company value). It was a big energizer for people, as well as helping to improve performance.

As a company, if you are going to go public with your values, live them authentically and consistently. On the occasions when you fail to meet expectations, be transparent and address the issues, and you will swiftly move on to a better place.

> 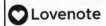**Lovenote**
>
> Clarifying your values gives you an internal compass to navigate how to make work better for you as an individual, for your team and for your company.

Freedom within a framework

Julie has been consistently described as the best boss by numerous team members over the years. From humble beginnings Julie has surpassed her own career expectations. She was the first member of her family to attend university, and along with her fierce intellect she has developed an exceptionally high emotional intelligence. In other words, Julie combines her cognitive capability with strong self-knowledge and self-regulation, as well as an ability to relate to and influence others. She has sought to blend her understanding of both business issues and people challenges, and this has put her in a resourceful position to anticipate and adapt to most scenarios. However, there is one value that Julie places ahead of all others – trust. Her starting point is to trust others until there is the evidence not to. This means that she creates environments where people have the autonomy to be self-directed. They are able to make decisions, act and keep improving, based on their results. They feel able to be themselves without fearing any negative consequences. It also means that Julie can be her authentic self and that she trusts herself to face situations with courage and conviction.

Contrast this with Sam who worked alongside Julie for several years. Sam's starting point was to *not* trust. He simply didn't trust anyone, even when they delivered consistently high performance year after year. His super-achieving team members admitted that they never felt fully trusted, and this was compounded by Sam's desire to go into minute detail, which would drive them to distraction. Sam ran his department on fear. He had a loud, threatening and aggressive style. Unfortunately, he reported to a boss who found it convenient to keep Sam in role, as his experience delivered short-term business performance which shareholders wanted.

Both these approaches achieved results. Both Julie and Sam were passionate about what they did, but they used very different work frameworks leading to different outcomes. A work framework shapes how you work. It sets your expectations, most of which are unconscious. Unless you deliberately define your framework, then you will be run by it unconsciously.

Angela Brav, President of Hertz International, shared her framework in our interview:

> We often tell young people to follow their heart when building a career. In my experience I don't know if we have the luxury to do everything we love. However, I do believe it's critical to find a way to love what we are doing. For instance, I led Information and Technology for a company. Technology was not my passion, but I focused on the difference I could make through developing a great team, ensuring everyone had a sense of belonging and creating an environment where people enjoyed coming to work. These factors helped unlock the potential of the technology experts who could thrive in a supportive workplace.

What is your framework? What are those non-negotiable factors that determine how you work? Growing up at a specialist music school shaped a considerable part of Ben's framework. Discipline, never giving up, continuous learning, collaborating with others and being inspired have been foundational elements of his code. However, the shadow side of these expectations means that Ben finds it hard to switch off. He gets frustrated when he sees what he interprets as laziness in others. He believes that whatever he does it's not enough and that he should be doing more. These are unhealthy traits, as they are subjective and can detract from Ben's love of what he does, as well as having the potential to disengage others from working with him. (Thankfully, Sophie rose above them!)

Your work framework defines how you work.

It's important to define your framework so that you can evaluate whether it's working for you or not by referring back to the most significant events that have shaped the way you work.

The following table shows an example of defining a work framework:

1 Event	2 Impact	3 Learning	4 Expectation
Working in the family business as a child	Shaped a work ethic that the majority of time should be dedicated to work and that work is a family affair	Working hard shows loyalty and commitment	A well-developed work ethic is a good thing, and anyone who is not prepared to go the distance is weak
Letting down a line manager by failing on a project, but being given a second chance	Feeling immense gratitude for the level of understanding and appreciation for having the opportunity to demonstrate healthy recovery	Assume good intent because it's extremely rare that anyone would deliberately fail	Work is about continuous learning, and showing insatiable curiosity goes a long way
Seeing others discriminated against and losing equal opportunities to succeed	Sense of injustice about bias and exclusion	Everyone has an equal right to belong, feel valued and fulfil their potential	Demonstrate inclusion and genuine appreciation of difference

Once you have defined your framework, you can then refine it to a few key points. Taking this example, this could boil down to:

- work ethic
- continuous improvement
- being inclusive.

This exercise gives you the opportunity to step back and evaluate your framework. Using the above example it could be helpful to reflect on the following questions:

- What is the impact of your work ethic? Does it nourish healthy discipline? Does it translate as useful perseverance? What is the risk of becoming obsessed by work and overworking to the point of it becoming detrimental to wellbeing, relationships and results?
- How do you blend continuous improvement with recognizing when enough is enough? Does continuous improvement energize others, or switch them off?
- How do you measure inclusion? What effect does your unconscious bias have on judging others' behaviour? How inclusive are you really?

A great example is the framework of Oliver Bonke, CEO, Middle East, Europe, India, Americas, of Shangri-La Hotels and Resorts. He is very clear about his three key elements, which he describes as energy, impact and momentum:

Energy is about reciprocity. To do the work I love I need to give and receive energy. It's important to know what gives you energy. It's different for everyone. Some people get energy out of clarity, chaos or empowerment of decision making. I do believe that as a leader you must give energy to the team and organization to help them do their best work. This will then come back to you in the results they deliver. I need to see that what I help lead creates impact which can be measured across multiple dimensions. To love my work I don't have to make a big impact, but it needs to be tangible so that I can touch, see and smell it! I need to be moving towards outcomes at pace while making material progress. I need to see momentum building towards meaningful benefits whether it is developing culture, solving crises or creating business development.

Someone else who has given considerable thought to what guides their work is Jamie Bunce, CEO of Inspired Villages, who shared the following insight:

I have always loved work. For instance, while at school I would be looking for ways to make things happen. From the unofficial tuck shop to double paper rounds, I always felt the need to work. From an early age I saw the positive in everything; for example my parents divorced when I was nine years old, I was obviously very upset, but quickly saw it is an opportunity to double my pocket money! I have never expected to get anything for free and have always been happy to work for my rewards. I love to see opportunities evolve. I get great enjoyment from seeing a direct physical result from my efforts, which naturally led me into the real-estate business.

Jamie has identified five steps to guide the work he loves:

1 Have a burning desire to do something in the form of a purpose.
2 Have a simple outlook to generate ideas and link them to business outcomes.
3 Have an eye for detail to see an issue or opportunity through the lens of others.
4 Have deep empathy to build meaningful long-term relationships.
5 Have the drive to make a tangible positive difference to people's lives.

Khaled Ismail, Vice President Communications, Europe, Central Asia, Middle East and Africa, at Tetra Pak, has given deep thought to his framework:

I wrote a book titled *This is What Tickles Me* based on observations from everyday moments and business life. So, there is a little bit of fun and many 'aha' moments which have contributed to my love of work. Having worked for two big companies, Coca-Cola and now Tetra Pak, I love achieving big things. For instance, holding the World Cup in my hands during France '98 and walking on the side lines of World Cup matches were special moments. I am driven to wake up every day and achieve something special. With Tetra Pak having the opportunity to give back in whichever way and contributing to making food safe and available everywhere gives me purpose. What takes away from my love of work is corporate jargon and bureaucracy mixed with individual egos where people think they are superior to you. Layers exist because that's how companies work, but with each layer comes some subjectivity and personal agendas. All of this reduces trust, effectiveness and the speed of decision making.

Everyone has a different framework. It's not black and white, and there is no such thing as right or wrong. The important element is raising awareness about yours, recognizing the impact that it has on others, seeking to understand other people's frameworks, and how you can gain alignment between them.

On occasion, we are invited to mediate between two parties to help seek mutual solutions, and to work with teams focused on drawing out a collective work framework. For instance, we were asked to facilitate a conversation between a high-profile supplier and customer. Before bringing the parties together, we met with each party to understand their context, outcomes and issues that needed to be resolved. The customer was accusing the supplier of being arrogant, failing to understand or engage with the customer's interests and not delivering on its promises. The supplier felt that the customer was hypercritical, demanding and excessive in its demands.

When we met, we allowed both parties to share their reality and seek to understand each other's perspectives. This began to ease the tension; however, the breakthrough came when we asked them to explain their individual work codes, in other words their expectations and how these were impacting the situation. The customer described its code as:

- Anticipate and surpass people's expectations.
- Challenge and be able to be challenged.
- Show how much you care.

The supplier shared its code:

- Have professional dialogue.
- Demonstrate respect.
- Energize others to get the best out of them.

Looking at their conflict through these lenses helped to iron out their differences. Each could both see how its behaviour might come across to the other. The supplier acknowledged that under the frame of professionalism and respect it could be experienced as distant and aloof. The customer could see that its expectation to go above and beyond in a challenging way could be interpreted as being demanding and excessive. Each party realized that both of them cared passionately and as a result they were able to co-create their own framework for working together:

- Make no assumptions.
- Have each other's back.
- Focus on win/win outcomes.

To keep things alive and real, they both committed to reviewing the state of their relationship regularly in addition to reviewing performance. We often see a large part of conflict in teams caused by a lack of clarity about what's been agreed around how they should work together. On one occasion, we worked with an operational leadership team responsible for a big-scale project. When we first met, they were under huge pressure and scrutiny to deliver on time and budget. Tensions were running high, and there were conflicting opinions about the solutions required to accelerate delivery. The team leader was known for his democratic style, which, although a strength, in this scenario added to the resistance, as some people just wanted to be told what to do. Having conducted a team diagnostic through conducting personal interviews to draw out key insights about what a work framework might look like, we brought the team together for an offsite workshop. There was a range of themes to address including:

- ensuring a shared sense of purpose
- having defined outcomes
- demonstrating collaborative ways of working
- acting at pace
- recognizing and celebrating success.

When we conduct this process with a team, we share the insights ahead of time, so that everyone is in the picture. When together, we ask people to identify their top three work expectations. Once we have collected all their ideas, we challenge people to vote for their number one. We have found that it is as important to have the conversation as it is to come up with a defined framework. We also apply what is known as the 'rule of three' to agree the final elements. The 'rule of three' is one way of focusing on the vital few to ensure that what is agreed sticks. (Research shows most people can remember three points easily.) In this instance, after rigorous debate the team landed on the following.

- Have an exciting plan.
- Get on with it.
- Ask for help.

Articulating the framework in plain language and keeping it simple is another important aspect of making it memorable and helping it stick.

Before you get busy working together, make sure you have clarified the work framework to keep you focused.

 **Lovenote**

Your framework sets clear expectations that will simplify and speed up doing great work with others.

Decision-making criteria

Grant was a seasoned executive approaching his fiftieth birthday. This milestone triggered a reflective process about how much he wanted to continue his existing path. Leading the commercial department in a global organization, Grant had surpassed his career expectations, but the demands had taken their toll on his health, wellbeing and family life. He approached us for some targeted coaching focused on creating the necessary clarity to make a decision about his next work chapter.

When somebody considers making external changes to their work, our starting point is to help them look closely at their internal motivations to ensure that they have clear decision-making criteria to guide their choices. Any criteria are intensely personal and are based on what they believe is right and true for them. We asked Grant to clarify what was most important for him to be able to make a definitive decision about what he wanted to do. He came up with ten key factors:

1 **Self** What does my authentic self look like in the next chapter of my work?

2 **Purpose** How do I want my deepest motivation to be fulfilled?

3 **Strengths** What will energize and strengthen me going forward?

4 **Responsibilities** What am I accountable for in the future?

5 **Relationship** Who do I want to spend time with?

6 **Family** How do I want to be involved with my family?

> **7 Reputation** What do I want to be known for?

> **8 Finance** How do I want my financial drive to influence me?

> **9 Growth** What do I want to learn and develop?

> **10 Contribution** What difference do I want to make?

These were big questions, and Grant needed time to reflect on them. Over the following months we kept closely in touch as he evolved his thinking. On the back of these criteria, Grant came up with several options:

- continuing in his existing role and maxing out for a limited amount of time
- staying in his existing role and negotiating flexible working hours
- moving to a smaller company in a commercial role, which would give him greater flexibility
- changing direction and applying his skills in different ways such as advising, teaching or working for a charity.

We encouraged Grant to tap into his network and engage in conversations to broaden his horizons. Getting advice from a range of people and sectors helped him define what mattered most. What emerged was the sense that he had one last significant role in him where he could bring together his learning, help people along the way and deliver big results. The most important people to gain alignment with were his family. He had sacrificed enough and was not prepared to repeat the past. Grant discussed the passion he felt for pursuing another opportunity and, together with his family, agreed the boundaries to make it work. He met with head-hunters to explore other opportunities. He looked at various roles until one came along that seemed to tick a lot of the boxes he was seeking. He went through numerous interviews, and each one seemed to nudge his thinking along. At the point of being offered a new role Grant stopped in his tracks. He realized that the biggest opportunity he had to reshape his future was in his existing role: he had a great track record; he knew how to get things done; he had strong working relationships. What had been missing was his open-mindedness to see and do things differently. Grant went to his boss to reset expectations. He shared his dilemma with her, together with his decision-making criteria and the support he needed going forward. His boss welcomed how far Grant had come, and they pledged to work together to shape his next chapter.

> Developing your criteria for work contextualizes your key decisions.

We loved the way Emily Chang, Chief Executive Officer, China, McCann Worldgroup, evolved her decision-making criteria, after taking a year out from her career to write a book, *The Spare Room*.

As the year drew to a close, I found myself at the proofing stage ... and wondering what I was going to do in the back half of my professional career, now that the book was moving into production. Would I write full time ... Should I go full-time into teaching and speaking? Or should I indulge my desire to live my social legacy, staying at home full-time and caring for vulnerable children with nowhere else to go? What about non-profit? Or back to one of the industries I had so enjoyed in the first half of my career? What an extraordinarily wide range of options to consider! How would I proceed?

I stepped back and evaluated the work I really love to do, and the environment in which I thrive. Most of us can survive in a job … but where did I find myself waking each morning in anticipation, and falling asleep each evening feeling intellectually and emotionally sated?

To help her in her decision she came up with a three-part model – Head–Heart–Soul:

Head: I realized that I do best when intellectually stimulated. I love to face into big, interesting challenges. And the one that keeps evolving, which intrigues me the most, was all about digital. It's about how the world has shifted from a place of pushed content to two-way engagement. From advertising to social dialogue. From TV films to online–offline integrated customer experiences. That was what I wanted to work on!

Heart: I love teaching and encouraging. Watching people develop and nurture their passions, build successful careers and thrive! I wanted to be in a place where I could help many people realize their aspirations and personal development goals.

Soul: Now that I had written a book on living a more intentional life and leading with authentic purpose, I felt more compelled than ever to find a company that shared that ethos. Where could I work where corporate values mirrored my own?

The Head–Heart–Soul framework proved crucial, leading her to her current job at McCann Worldgroup, where she got to work for a company that 'lives by a mantra that truly inspires me': 'When I heard that the corporate values were BIG (B = Bravery. I = Integrity. G = Generosity), I was sold.'

This is a great example of how company values can act as a lighthouse, creating a beam of light to guide employees whose own values chime with theirs. Emily heartily believes that developing a framework as she did can transform your relationship with work: 'What's the framework that can help you do the same? I'd encourage you to step away from the standard parameters – of preferred industry, region or title. Rather, pull out a blank sheet of paper and begin writing down what really matters to you, and see where the exercise takes you!'

It's essential to keep an open mind when creating the criteria to inform your decision-making process. As Richard Solomons, Chairman of Rentokil, described in our interview:

> It's important to separate financial success from traditional career success so that you broaden your measures of success. I have noticed that many people at the top of their professions are quite narrow in their outlook. Get your head around what you love and what fulfils you. People still go on to me about having been a CEO but it's irrelevant. Some external calibration is OK, but it isn't why I do what I do. At the end of the day figure out what you want to do and follow it.

Joel Burrows, CEO at Ghirardelli, gave us his advice about how 'to figure out what you love about work':

> Set aside time to think about it. You will need to make a deliberate attempt to understand what motivates and drives you. Ask yourself, what are you about as a human being? What are your intrinsic motivations? What makes you happy? What do you want from life? Once you have some deeper insight then reflect upon what you specifically like doing. For example is it solving problems on your own, or working on projects in groups?
>
> On a personal note my intrinsic motivation which I describe as my purpose is 'to create real relationships and help others to enjoy and be at their best'. In a work context this plays out through my love of people and numbers. For instance, I love Monday morning because I get excited to see how our sales have performed over the weekend! I also love discussing succession planning and seeing how to help other people learn and grow. Once you have some clarity about your motivation you will need to have real conversations with others and get feedback about when they see you energized and at your best.

Another similar perspective comes from Renée Elliott, founder of Planet Organic and co-founder of Beluga Bean, who shared:

> If you're at a stage of thinking what's next in your work, be mindful about why you want to change. Are you being driven by the wrong things, for

instance ego and blind ambition? My criteria for decision making include trusting my inner voice, not compromising myself, respecting myself and keeping my boundaries. I encourage people to prioritize factors like health, happiness, psychological, emotional and economic wellbeing, and being engaged with a spiritual practice that calms you. Failing to respect these elements puts you at risk of getting off track. It's essential to have good communication with yourself so that when you feel off centre, you're able to tell yourself the truth. Why did I slip? What do I need to do to correct it? If you are in a thoughtful place, you won't go into overwork and your work will be an expression of your highest self.

Making the right decision about your work is an intensely personal matter. We suggest reflecting on the following areas to challenge your thinking:

1 How can my work be a reflection of my purpose?

2 What inspires me the most in work?

3 How can my work be an expression of my values?

4 What strengthens and energizes me about work?

5 How do I want to stretch, learn and grow?

6 What does my ambition look like in work?

7 What kind of work do I want to be involved with?

8 What type of people do I want to spend time with?

9 What kind of industry excites me?

10 Which type of company do I care for?

11 What reputation do I want to have?

12 How do I want to contribute in meaningful ways?

Answers to such questions can become the criteria that guide your work. They ensure that you have clarity about what is most important and that you focus on what matters most. When your work is an expression of your innate wisdom, it will uplift you and you will flourish in ways you probably cannot predict today. Do the work on yourself to have clarity and you will be rewarded in multiple ways. As John Holland-Kaye, CEO of Heathrow, expresses it:

If you love what you do you are usually doing what you love. Don't do something that makes you unhappy. Find what inspires you. There are people in companies who are radiators or drains. The drains and zappers are unhappy in their work. The radiators and energizers are inspired and do what they love. I have found that those who are most unhappy in their work are on a wage where they can't afford to leave and feel trapped. This in turn means that they can become a blocker to others who want to move up. Part of the role of a leader is to make sure they create the opportunities where people can move around, not get caught in a wage trap and do what they love.

Let's reinforce Holland-Kaye's point about the impact that leaders have with an important perspective from Tetra Pak's Khaled Ismail:

For those working in companies the challenge to love or not to love your work comes down to an important point: people don't leave companies, they leave managers. There is no doubt that if you are working for someone who is able to get the best out of you then it will help you love your work. On the other hand, if you experience work as a grind and your manager is condescending, harsh and unfair, then it compounds the problem … if a person is able to lead others in a way that gets the best out of them then they can help them love their work.

He went on to pinpoint how a great leader can help others love their work in three ways:

1 **Provide clear direction** – help people to understand the purpose of their work and how it is linked to the delivery of the business.
2 **Create a safe environment** – don't let people fear failure and don't create a culture of fear.
3 **Give autonomy** – give people the space to succeed by not micromanaging but backing them up when they need support.

When you define your decision-making criteria, make sure working with a great leader is a high priority.

Another element to consider is how well you know yourself. Sam Barrell, COO of the Francis Crick Institute, put it this way:

It is essential to follow something that interests you. Write down what you like and don't like in work ... Make sure that you talk to people, research websites, speak to HR teams and get a proper feel for what particular roles are really like. Engage with as many people working in different roles as you can to learn about what they do, why they do it and what they love about it. Think about your skills – list them; what attracts you to various roles and how can you match your skills with them? Get to understand yourself better. Conduct research on yourself! It's an intensive project.

Graham Alexander, Founder of The Alexander Partnership, shared some practical ideas that you can use to evaluate your work criteria. First, 'see clearly what you love to do and hate what you do in your current work', then 'focus on how you can do more of what you love and less of what you hate'. When you have done so, he suggests three options:

1 Stop some things. Evaluate what is not valuable for you or the organization (e.g. unnecessary bureaucracy).
2 Find someone who is better than you to do things (e.g. delegate what you can).
3 Learn to work more efficiently to reduce the time on what you dislike (e.g. put tight deadlines on specific tasks only you can do).

His practical advice continued:

For those in roles, ask yourself, 'If I really loved this job, what would it look like?' For those considering a role, evaluate it through the lens of clarity, confidence and commitment. Ask yourself on a scale of 1–10 where 1 represents very low and 10 represents very high:

1 How clear am I about what I need to accomplish?

2 How confident am I in my ability to achieve that?

3 How committed am I to making it happen?

Then look at the answers with low scores and ask yourself what you need to do to move forward.

Building upon this insight, we suggest clarifying your criteria to progress your ideal work. Be open-minded about what it could look like. Allow serendipity to play a part. Don't forget to prioritize factors such as health, emotional, relational, psychological, economic and spiritual wellbeing for long-term sustainability. And above all, make sure your criteria inspires and excites you to move you in the direction you want to go.

❤ **Lovenote**

What's your criteria for thriving at work? Set these clearly to enable high-velocity decision making.

At the heart of it

Clarifying your personal code is one of
the most exciting and important things you can do.

Think of this as a treasure hunt,
with your values, decision-making criteria and framework as
powerful clues, helping you on the adventure
towards doing what you love.

STAGE 2

Develop

So far during our *LoveWork* journey we have covered the Discover stage of the 3D Model, focusing on the analysis and insight we need to create the foundations of self-knowledge:

- Our **first step** (Chapter 1) looked at 'why' (defining your purpose).
- Our **second step** (Chapter 2) articulated your 'what' (your inspiring vision and the direction you want to go).
- The **third step** (Chapter 3) was about uncovering your code – your 'how'.

We now move on to Stage 2: Develop, which provides the opportunity for you to test and challenge your thinking to expand your impact and influence.

4
Activate momentum

How strengths strengthen you

The global strengths movement started six decades ago when Don Clifton, creator of CliftonStrengths, posed a simple question: 'What would happen if we studied what was right with people versus what's wrong with people?' He wrote: 'There is no more effective way to empower people than to see each person in terms of his or her strengths.'

Marcus Buckingham, creator of the Standout Strengths Assessment, clarified what strengths actually are and are not:

Strengths are not something that you're good at, just like weaknesses aren't something that you're bad at. A strength is an activity that strengthens you. That you look forward to doing. It's an activity that leaves you feeling energized, rather than depleted. We all have things that we're good at, but that we hate doing, right? Those are called weaknesses. A strength is more appetite than ability, and it's that appetite that drives us to want to do it again; practise more; refine it to perfection. The appetite leads to the practice, which leads to performance. Leveraging your strengths and managing around your weaknesses isn't just about making yourself feel better. It's about conditioning yourself to contribute the best of yourself, every day. It's about performance. Every one of us has unique strengths. And every one of us will contribute more when we take our strengths seriously, and intelligently leverage them for the benefit of the world.

Playing to strengths was a common theme in our interviews: people had either deliberately led with strengths and/or focused on helping others be strengths-based. Keith Barr, CEO of IHG, highlighted his perspective on the importance of focusing on strengths and being energized:

> To do the work you love it's vital to understand what gives you energy. Ask yourself: What gives you energy? I have found that what people often miss is having a better understanding of who they are, what gives them energy and what helps them to have a sense of purpose and accomplishment. Recognize that if you are taking a job for the title, or for the money, it won't be sustainable in the long run.

Angela Brav, President of Hertz International, reinforced this view:

> People often don't realize the power of passion and playing to strengths. For instance, if you don't always have the right answers it doesn't matter because unlocking passion and strengths will bring out the best in others and together you will get to the right solutions. For instance, I believe I am passionate about showing people that what they do matters and that you care. Coming into Hertz I was determined to initially lead with this strength, so rather than putting my primary attention on the strategy and delivering the plan, I focused on connecting with people and my engagement scores were outstanding simply by showing people who they are and what they do matters. My messaging was clear: I am not in the car business, I am in the people business. We need you, and you make us better.

When developing others to discover their strengths and leverage them in their careers, Angela will use a variety of questions to gain greater clarity about where they are going, including:

What can you bring that nobody else can bring?

What can you add to this job that nobody else can do?

What energy can you bring that nobody else has?

How can you transform this space so customers love it?

How can you bring yourself into an environment and know that you have made a difference?

How can you signal that you have left a bit of yourself in what you do?

How can you create the best version of yourself in work?

Emma Gilthorpe, COO at Heathrow Airport, is focused on spotting strengths in others and the impact it can have on recruitment:

> My approach is to recruit will, train skill … If you get a motivated person who has the right attitude and work ethic and is a true collaborator, then it's far more important than their skillset. I have found that collaborative, motivated and energetic people overcome most situations. In fact, sometimes having technical skills can be a hurdle because they can act as a blocker to collaboration or visualizing a shared outcome. I would pick an unqualified, motivated person over a technical, low-energy person any day.

Laura Miller, Executive Vice President, Chief Information Officer at Macy's, shared valuable insight about linking strengths to career progression:

Your work progression is directly linked with playing to your strengths as you simply wouldn't progress if you are playing to your weaknesses! However, throughout my career the majority of training I received in companies was focused on trying to fix my weaknesses. I believe it's important to make sure that your weaknesses don't become derailers, but your focus should be on playing to your strengths. I have also found that over-indexing on your strengths helps others be more forgiving about your weaknesses. Working on your strengths is fun and is based on what you love to do.

Staynton Brown, Director Diversity and Inclusion and Talent at Transport for London, put forward his view in our interview:

People thrive when they focus on what they can do. For instance, taking a strengths-based approach it is always best to try to put people in positions where they can succeed. There is no doubt that we need challenge. However, people respond better to appreciation and an approach that gives them energy. Being strengths-based and energy-led fires people up. This needs to be managed alongside clear and honest feedback so that people have the right language to understand what good looks like.

So what are your strengths? There are some great online tools to help you discover your strengths including CliftonStrengths Assessment and StandOut® Strengths Assessment. However, to start your inquiry, you should reflect on the various activities you are involved with and the impact on your energy. What energizes and strengthens you? What de-energizes and drains you? What patterns and links do you notice that equate to a strength – that is, an activity that strengthens you, you want to do and leaves you feeling energized.

> Play to your strengths and you will become stronger in your work.

The following table shows examples of activities that energize/ de-energize and their links to potential strengths:

Activity	Insight	Strengths
Delivering a project	Energized by the challenge of being deadline driven, overcoming roadblocks and delivering tangible outcomes De-energized by 'office politics', seeking consensus and indecision	Execution Pace Focus Drive
Working collaboratively	Energized by being part of a team, creating joint solutions and making things better as a result of partnership. De-energized by silo ways of working, big egos and personal agendas	Empathy Connector Harmonizer Relational
Developing strategy	Energized by thinking ahead, conducting scenario planning and seeking causes/reasons De-energized by lack of sound theories, unclear patterns and outcomes	Analytical Planner Learner Futuristic
Leading teams	Energized by inspiring others, unlocking performance and developing talent De-energized by negativity, lack of accountability and action	Influencer Communication Development Activation

Reinforce your self-reflection by seeking feedback from others. Ask people from a range of touch points including family, friends, colleagues and clients about their experience of you. When do they see you energized? De-energized? What strengths do they think you possess and when do they see you playing to them? See how the feedback you receive mirrors your own self-awareness.

Once you have a better idea about your strengths explore how you can use them every day. As we referenced earlier, the ADP Research Institute (ADPRI) conducted research in 2019 drawing on over 19,000 workers across the globe to measure levels of engagement and identify optimal conditions at work. One of the most relevant findings was: 'When a worker has the chance to use their strengths every day at work it builds trust with their team leader' (ADPRI, 2019).

Hence, if you are leading others, it's essential to identify the strengths of your team members and learn to play to them. Communicate your intent to create an environment where everyone can play to their strengths every day. Set up dedicated conversations with each team member on an individual basis to clarify their strengths and agree how they can use them every day. Offer to give them consistent feedback on where you see them playing to their strengths, the impact of those strengths and how they can leverage them more.

Robert was a strengths-based leader. He instinctively knew that it was the right approach to take and was passionate about maximizing the potential of his team. Robert had engaged us to work with him to develop his leadership team. We dedicated one of our early sessions to the issue of playing to strengths. The majority of the team had worked together over time so had a good appreciation of each other's strengths and weaknesses. We asked them to reflect on and discuss the business case for strengths.

The majority of the team resonated with the concept of playing to strengths and identified the following benefits. Playing to strengths:

- increases effectiveness and productivity as it gets the best out of people
- unlocks potential for better performance by tapping into people's intrinsic motivation
- improves energy and engagement, helping to create a positive work environment
- leads to better collaboration as team members cover each other's weaknesses and have each other's backs.

However, they also called out the risks of overused strengths including:

- being too forceful with an idea or point of view, which can cause disengagement
- adopting a fixed mindset as a result of having a narrow outlook
- failing to collaborate effectively
- overlooking others' contributions due to being overly focused on self.

We discussed the impact of mitigating weaknesses and how, when you are caught in situations where you are weak, you become drained and de-energized. Robert was candid with the team about his weaknesses such as navigating company politics, generating polished presentations and seeking credit for great results. The team could see the risk of working in an environment that did not mitigate weaknesses and face into them. For instance, Robert shared that he couldn't avoid company politics but that he needed to download his frustrations about its negative impact with the team so that it didn't weigh him down and he could reset himself when needed.

In the session we gave team members the opportunity to reflect on their own strengths and then conducted a feedback exercise where everyone gave and received views about their experience of each other using the following statements:

I see you playing to your strengths when …

I see you managing your weaknesses when …

We encouraged people, on receiving feedback, to simply acknowledge it by saying 'thank you' and to avoid getting into any immediate debate. By the time people had heard feedback from the whole team, themes had emerged for them to consider. We then give them time to debrief with a coaching partner to consolidate their insight. The final step was to hear insight from each team member about the main strength and weakness identified. It was extremely valuable as a team to gain a shared perspective so that they could increase their support of each other going forward.

We also asked everyone to describe their strengths as a collective, focused on when they experienced the team playing to its strengths. The strengths that emerged as a team were:

- **Trust** – they had inherent trust for each other and gave each other the autonomy to perform.
- **Confidence** – their performance was based on a fundamental belief that they could and would deliver their targets.
- **Adaptability** – they thrived in an environment of change and could flex their approach accordingly.
- **Realism** – as an operational team they were grounded in the reality of the myriad issues they faced, while always focused on solutions.
- **Resilience** – they had an amazing ability to bounce back from setbacks and the ongoing adversity they encountered.

The team was energized by focusing on its strengths. Members wanted to explore what it would mean to be more strengths-oriented when addressing their key priorities which included delivering a world-class customer experience, inspiring their teams, managing safety and creating an inclusive environment. It opened up different types of conversation and encouraged them to generate solutions which they hadn't considered before. For instance, they launched a strengths-based 360-degree feedback tool. This sent a positive message to their own teams in terms of playing to strengths and provided welcome relief for people who had become worn down by the constant focus on managing their weaknesses.

There is no doubt that playing to strengths as an individual, team or organization is one of the most effective ways of activating momentum on your journey to loving what you do and doing what you love.

 **Lovenote**

Energy and motion come from using our strengths. Identify and deploy them in the right way every day.

Blockers and barriers

What is your potential to do great work? What is your potential to optimize your performance? How can you fulfil your potential? These are big questions and, used in the right way, can inspire you to thrive in new and meaningful ways. At the heart of our work is a core hypothesis based on the following concept:

> Performance equals potential less interference.

In other words, by identifying and reducing interference you achieve a closer relationship between potential and performance.

Susan had recently been promoted to become the COO in a global organization. It was a fantastic opportunity for Susan which recognized her outstanding leadership and executional strengths. However, when we sat down with her to plan her first 90 days in role, she identified over a dozen possible roadblocks that could prevent her from bridging the gap between potential and performance. We grouped the roadblocks into three different areas:

1 the creation of a vision
2 engagement with stakeholders
3 the delivery of some quick wins.

We asked Susan to reflect on whether she had the potential to perform in these areas, and there was no question that she had the capability and track record to succeed. Nonetheless, she felt that there was a lot getting in her way, so we needed to dig deeper to help identify and eliminate this interference. To do so, we used one of our favourite coaching tools, 'The Structure of a Problem', which helps people move from a 'problem state' to a 'project state'. The steps are:

1 Describe the current reality of a situation.
2 Paint a picture of the desired result.
3 Name the different roadblocks to overcome.
4 Identify where they are located: (a) internal; (b) other(s); or (c) external.
5 Create a plan for the way forward.

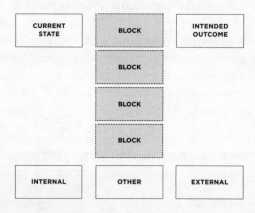

Coaching tool: Structure of a Problem

Continuing the coaching with Susan, we applied the tool to each area. When focusing on the first problematic area, 'the creation of a vision', she articulated the following:

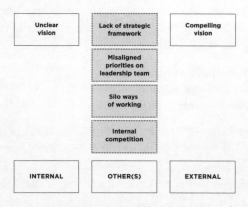

Coaching tool: Structure of a Problem (Susan)

When Susan reflected upon where the roadblocks were located, she realized that they sat in the 'Other' bucket. This meant that her priority was to focus on stakeholder management with her team, peers and line manager. Thankfully, this was one of Susan's strengths, and she felt confident that she could conduct the right process to create a compelling vision.

We recommend using this tool as a way of breaking down your thinking when you are faced with a challenge to overcome. We have learned *that the presenting issue is rarely the real issue.* In other words, when people come to you with a problem to solve, it's vital to suspend judgement until you have uncovered the root cause, especially when faced with organizational, team or individual performance issues. For instance, if an organization is failing to optimize performance, there could be a range of issues including brand equity, customer experience, right leadership, stakeholder engagement, organizational structure, sufficient resource, clear prioritization, governance … We could go on. Investing time in identifying what's really going on accelerates the unlocking of potential.

Another approach to unlocking potential comes from Stephen McCall, CEO of edyn, who in our interview highlighted four steps to take:

1 **Be clear about who you are and what you want** Figure out who you are and what you love. It's essential to think hard about the type of environment, organization and role you are suited to. For example, I designed my new role based on the following factors: I needed more creativity, control, the ability to move things faster and to work with a boutique brand. When I went out looking, I almost lost heart, but I stayed focused on what I wanted, and my current role came along.

2 **Be bold** It's important to have the courage to stay with the process. For instance, doing what you love might involve sacrificing some initial financial and reputational benefits. Do your due diligence and then have a leap of faith. If you're not happy, you will need to be prepared to take big decisions, and this takes courage. By examining what you are prepared to do and not do, then clarity will emerge. At the end of the day there are two main choices to make – deep change or slow death.

3 Be relational If you're in a role you love and following your passion, it will be hard to fail unless it has highly technical requirements which you are not equipped to take on. I have noticed that most organizations still cling on to a belief that technical capability is really important. However, over the last decade we have been moving from technical skills to things like intuition, impact and influence. In recruiting, I rarely worry about technical capability. It is a lot harder to build relationship at all levels in an organization, have a point of view, process information and rapidly cut through to decisions than it is to learn technical skills. You need to understand the economics and mechanics of how a business works, but how you get along with others is the most essential skillset.

4 Be a better version of you I started out from a job where on the face of it I should have been happy. It was an interesting industry, and I was in a highly leveraged position but not happy. I am now in a place where I have less status, but I'm much happier. I'm healthier, kinder and less arrogant, and I sleep better. I'm fundamentally a better person and no longer need to worry about being in the wrong fit. I firmly believe that enjoying what you do makes you a better person. Doing what you love is a life-changing event, and I believe it is beholden on everyone to unlock their potential to make it happen. Given the amount of time we spend at work, enjoying just half of what we do means we will have a life well lived.

Nick Dent, Director Customer Operations at London Underground, has multiple barriers to overcome working in a highly pressured operational environment while managing key priorities like safety and reliability:

Doing great work takes relentless determination. I like to build coalitions around big, complex challenges to align people around a shared vision and set of outcomes. It's vital to be clear about what you are trying to achieve and why. It is then important to be empathetic to understand why blockers and barriers exist. Although it is an investment of time, you need to bring people with you rather than deny any concerns. It takes resilience as you are usually dealing with deeply rooted cultural issues which can't be resolved in a day.

Activating momentum requires the ability to break down barriers in ways that help you and others do your best work.

> ## ♥ Lovenote
>
> You will always find barriers on your journey. Working around
> them, overcoming them or removing them is a fundamental
> part of going faster and further at work.

Flow

In our interview with the psychologist Amy Edmondson, she referenced the research of Mihaly Csikszentmihalyi, one of the co-found-
ers of positive psychology:

> Csikszentmihalyi studied states in which people reported feelings of
> concentration and deep enjoyment. His studies revealed that what makes
> work genuinely satisfying is 'flow' – a state of concentration so focused
> that it amounts to complete absorption in an activity and results in the
> achievement of an ideal state of happiness. I believe that flow occurs when
> our skills and capabilities are balanced with the challenge of our work.

In *Flow: The Psychology of Optimal Experience*, Mihaly Csikszentmihalyi writes: 'The best moments usually occur when a person's body or
mind is stretched to its limits in a voluntary effort to accomplish something difficult and worthwhile. For each person there are thousands of
opportunities, challenges to expand ourselves' (Csikszentmihalyi, 1990).
When did you last experience a state of flow? What contributed
to being in flow? How often do you deliberately cultivate flow? We
find writing an opportunity to be in flow when our skills are blended
with the challenge of articulating ideas in a clear and compelling way.
We are stretched to our limits to accomplish something difficult and
worthwhile. We often encounter people who say they would love to
write a book. We have written 12 between us and have found that
each book helps move us forward.

All feats of greatness are rooted in the opportunity to be in flow. From
the world of sports comes the enthralling documentary *Last Dance* about
the extraordinary basketball career of Michael Jordan. In his final game at

Madison Square Garden playing for Chicago Bulls, Michael Jordan put on a pair of 14-year-old Chicago Air Jordan 1s that were a size too small. By half time, his feet were bleeding, but he was playing so well he was loathe to take them off. It's interesting to note that Michael Jordan credits sports psychologist and mindful meditation teacher George Mumford with helping unlock his potential and get into the 'zone'. In an interview with ABC News, George Mumford described one of his approaches with athletes. 'They know what "the zone" is, they know what "being in flow" is, so when I talk about that, they're all ears.'

In the world of business, Steve Jobs embodied living in the 'zone'. In his 2011 biography of the Apple founder, Walter Isaacson described how Job's intensity manifested itself in his ability to focus: 'It honed his appreciation for intuition, showed him how to filter out anything that was distracting or unnecessary, and nurtured in him an aesthetic based on minimalism' (Isaacson, 2011).

It's fascinating how entrepreneur Elon Musk creates his 'zone'. Among the quotations which capture his approach is this one: 'When something is important enough, you do it even if the odds are not in your favour.'

If we follow the premise of Amy Edmondson that flow occurs when your skills and capabilities are balanced with the challenge of your work, then how can you create the conditions to inspire flow? What are your specific skills and capabilities to utilize? What is the challenge in your work you can tap into?

> Being in flow equates to loving your work.

Paul Snyder, Executive Vice President Stewardship, at the Tillamook County Creamery Association, shared his thoughts on this subject:

When you love what you do there is a resonance and an experience of being in the flow. For instance, in some of my first sustainability projects

I felt like I was being who I was meant to be. It became self-fulfilling. I wanted more of this feeling. I suggest doing an inventory of what makes you feel at your best. What I discovered was focusing on bringing together sustainability, social justice and making business a force for good in the world translated into being the best version of me.

Errol Williams, Vice President at WeWork, discussed his view about setting up the conditions for flow at work:

I am influenced by a quote from Ecclesiastes 3:13: 'And also that every man should eat and drink, and enjoy good in all his labour, is the gift of God.' I have come to think that it's not our jobs that are so critical, but our ability to find enjoyment in our work that matters. My philosophy is to take your unique talents, personality, interests and life goals and then find work that provides enjoyment given these. This requires an honest assessment about blending your talents and interests to discover the options that make the most sense for you. Obviously, I understand the need to provide the right income and lifestyle for our family. However, I have consistently sought out work that has engaged my talent, personality and has provided real enjoyment.

In our interview with Wim Dejonghe, Senior Partner at Allen & Overy, he reflected on how his leadership responsibilities help him to be in the 'zone':

I ask myself, 'What can I do professionally to make a difference in people's lives?' For instance, my primary concern during COVID-19 was the responsibility to look after the 6,000 families of all of our people. I took to writing regular blogs to share my thinking with colleagues and received amazing stories in return which reinforced my belief in doing the right thing for our people by making a connection with them. I also recognize that I can make a big difference for my clients. While I have been accused of having an overdeveloped sense of responsibility, this is just how I'm wired and it's what keeps me going. Certainly, in times of crisis I am confident of being the right person to steer the ship and I take pleasure in seeing people forming a strong team around me.

Being in flow activates momentum by ensuring you are in the zone on a more frequent basis, thereby generating massive energy for thriving at work.

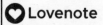

Lovenote

To flourish at work, find your flow.

Progress versus perfection

We have so far looked at how playing to strengths, overcoming blockers and barriers, and being in flow helps to activate momentum. Another critical ingredient to develop is an approach of continuous improvement to nudge yourself forward day to day. We love the idea of making a better tomorrow built on a philosophy of progress versus perfection.

One leader we coached who was committed to driving continuous improvement was James. He was brought in to run the central operations function in a complex business. Historically, the department was known for operating in a siloed way with highly directive leadership. However, given the increasing interdependencies within the business, this approach was not sustainable for future success. It was critical that the function became joined up with the rest of the organization through shared priorities and working in collaborative ways. James was selected for a skillset that matched a lot of the conditions required. He was anchored in a strong sense of purpose. He derived his energy from achieving big goals, which was just as well as he was now leading over 4,000 colleagues in a heavily unionized environment. He collaborated in a way that ensured people felt understood and influenced others to act in democratic ways. He was wired to take initiative and invested heavily in creating robust plans to provide clarity for the way ahead. One of his main skills was a commercial focus, which added another dimension in an operational environment that needed to become more efficient and affordable. However, one of the primary reasons he was right for this role was the way he constantly sought opportunities to do things differently and make improvements for the better.

Coming into the role was a big challenge for James, as he adjusted to the cut and thrust of a daily operational environment which stretched his endurance. However, he found himself in the flow as he became deeply absorbed in the existential challenges the business demanded. We supported James in bringing his leadership team together and helped lay the foundations for how they would work together going forward. Barriers were broken down, trust was formed and eyes were lifted up to the future. Moving from the relentless day-to-day delivery to a more strategic way of thinking and working exercised different muscles for the team, and this was initially uncomfortable. James persisted with his focus and made himself fully available for coaching conversations with team members to support their transition. Not everyone made it, but those who did were encouraged to identify their skills to leverage and began to thrive on the challenge.

The team formed a compelling narrative about the direction they were heading to share with the business. A key message was about 'being open for business', signalling a strong intent to collaborate in joined-up ways. They ran workshops to co-create what future operations could look like with colleagues from across the business. Gradually, there was a perception shift in the company to seeing operations as genuinely being at the heart of the business where everyone wanted to be involved. James later described the experience as a career highlight. Although he had taken the role with trepidation about what it might involve, it unlocked his potential and developed his ability.

> Your capability is not fixed. You can always become a better version of you.

We use a '4P' model to explore capability:

'4P' model	Principles	People	Process	Profit
	How you communicate and make decisions	How you inspire and engage others	How you drive for results in an effective way	How you use commercial acumen to help growth
Capability:	Being purpose-led	Listening to understand	Using initiative	Anticipating opportunity
	Leading with values	Seeking win/win outcomes	Taking accountability	Setting clear success criteria
	Being inclusive	Adapting personal style	Being decisive	Making trade-offs
	Playing to strengths	Collaborating effectively	Putting plans in place	Being efficient
	Inspiring through vision	Influencing others to act	Taking action	Driving results

- **Principles** What are your guiding principles that provide a decision-making framework and ensure you come across in a consistent way? In our experience it is rare to come across people who have given sufficient thought to their principles and are known for what they stand for. Factors to consider include being purpose-led, values-based, inclusive, strengths-based and inspiring through vision.
- **People** How do you inspire and engage others? Having strong people ability means building effective relationships based on trust and mutual understanding. It requires you to seek win/win outcomes, adapt your style to meet others' needs, collaborate effectively and influence others to act. The fundamental ingredient for having high people capability is emotional intelligence. This mix of self-awareness,

self-management, social awareness and social skills becomes a differentiator in whatever form of work you undertake.

- **Process** It's all very well having great vision and being able to get on with people. If, however, you can't deliver results with an effective process, then there will be question marks about your general capability. We have found that the ability to deliver and get stuff done at pace is point of entry in a work context. Others simply expect you to achieve results, at which point you have the licence to have a seat at the table.

- **Profit** We do not advocate profit without purpose; equally, we don't encourage purpose without profit (unless you are in an organization where for some reason this is entirely irrelevant; this is unusual, however, as even in a not-for-profit organization revenue and the financial or commercial situation play their role). For many, the sweet spot is your ability to contribute to financial growth in a purposeful way. This requires you to anticipate opportunity, set clear success criteria, make the right trade-offs, be efficient and drive results.

Whatever your strengths and weaknesses in relation to these 4Ps, capability is not fixed. You can continuously learn, grow, develop and become a better version of you.

Someone who has constantly challenged himself to expand their capability is Barry Robinson, President and Managing Director of International Operations at Wyndham Destinations, who recognizes that becoming a better version of yourself is a lifelong journey:

In the past I was very ambitious and focused on the next bigger and better hotel to operate. As the hospitality business has evolved, so have I. I love to be continually challenged and the reward of seeing people and the business develop together. I enjoy the chase of doing a deal which contributes to the overall strategy of the business and the flexibility of being creative when building a resort. It's important to ask yourself, 'Am I constructively challenging myself about how I am advancing?' You need to cultivate reflection within yourself and encourage honest feedback from others so that you are not being told what you want to hear. Then focus on constantly reinventing yourself so that you are able to evolve.

We welcomed the perspective of psychologist Amy Edmondson with her challenging perspective on capability:

> I want to be radical here … forget talent. Talent is a construct that we have made up to say some people are better than others. The reality is that we are better than each other on different dimensions. The raw material is nothing in comparison to healthy systems and structures in place combined with people who listen, are respectful and let you do great work. The war for talent in the 1990s was largely misleading. It let leaders off the hook from the impact of their own actions. The role of a leader is to create the conditions where ordinary people can do extraordinary things. As a leader, if you don't get people, your company won't perform well.

Whatever stage of work you are currently experiencing – for example, seeking a new opportunity, wanting a shift in a current role, looking to progress in your existing company – developing your capability can only be of benefit. We suggest the following three-step process:

1 What skills do you want to enhance? Identify the critical capability you need to learn and grow. Use the 4Ps as a lens to specify a few vital areas to accelerate your progress.
2 What challenges are you facing? Be clear about the primary interference you are experiencing that, if reduced or eliminated, would give you the biggest boost in your work.
3 Who can help you? You will only be as successful as your support network. Be prepared to reach out and ask those with greater skills and experience than you to advise and counsel you on how to become a better version of you.

As Richard Solomons, Chairman of Rentokil, put it in our interview:

> There is a lot of truth in the saying that success is 99 per cent perspiration and 1 per cent inspiration. I notice that drive is often born out of necessity. For instance, coming from a background of adversity, or needing to prove yourself, tends to create an internal drive. When you look at the top of professions the difference between the talent of the really top people and others is small. For example, in motor racing it can be the difference

between one second per lap, which is down to a combination of hard work and innate skill. Lewis Hamilton has both. If you want to be effective at what you do, it's about how you calibrate your passion, drive and talent.

Richard recognizes the role that skills play combined with hard work and drive. When you mix these with a big career challenge, it gives you the opportunity to thrive. If you are committed to unlocking your potential and becoming a better version of you, it will require you to stretch yourself in ways you have probably not yet considered.

♥ Lovenote

Be aware of the exponential effect of the incremental: 1 per cent improvement daily, compounded, is 3,800 per cent improvement annually. Drive small improvements to make big progress.

At the heart of it

Now is the time to get moving, to speed things up and to activate momentum.

Let's look at the physics of this.

Technically, momentum is calculated as mass multiplied by velocity.

(Velocity is speed in the right direction).

The structure you've built
of 'why', 'what' and 'how' allows you to know
that when you're moving at pace,
it's in the right direction.

Move with velocity.
And make sure that the movement delivers momentum.

Scientifically speaking, momentum happens
only when energy is introduced
(think of the explosive charge needed to fire a bullet).

Play to your strengths, unlock your potential,
get in flow and aim for progress over perfection –
these will give you the firepower for acceleration.

5
Give and get

Relationship intelligence

Steve was President of the Americas for a global hospitality company. He oversaw several thousand hotels, generated 75 per cent of the company profit, led thousands of people and had a big industry profile. He was busy. Steve was passionate about leadership development, and we were fortunate in that he always carved out precious time to support our leadership development programmes. He was meticulously prepared, having requested details on each delegate, and would show up having done his homework. One of his remarkable skills was to learn the name of each person along with an individual accomplishment so that when he greeted them it had a long-lasting effect. His personal touch created a lifetime memory for people as he was genuinely thoughtful and caring in his approach.

Steve would typically join us before dinner and conduct a 'fireside chat'. Whereas most leaders were quite scripted, Steve loved to share stories. He went around the whole group asking each person what question they would like to ask him – the more personal the better. He made a note of every question and would spend the course of the evening answering them through his stories. On one occasion a participant asked Steve, 'How do you spend your time? What do you do?' Without hesitation Steve responded: 'I simply spend time meeting people and telling them about the great work they do!' Steve was very clear that his primary value and role for the company was relationship-based. He was guided by the question everyone should be clear about: 'What can only I do?' For instance, Steve knew that, because of his position, he was the main person to build certain relationships and unlock value for the company.

> Business is relationship.

How do you prioritize relationships at work? What is your relationship plan? How deliberate are you in building great relationships to enhance your work? We find many people fail to consciously develop their relationships as they perceive doing this to be manipulative or inauthentic. This is only true if you make it so. Prioritizing and building great relationships is an essential element of creating the work you love, but developing an approach to how you are going to do it often gets overlooked. It doesn't mean having to spend endless hours sipping lukewarm chardonnay at networking events.

Angela Brav, President of Hertz International, describes her approach in the following way:

> I go out of my way to connect with my team, which ranges from colleagues at the front desk who give customers car keys to my direct reports to my executive peers. I make it my business to know how people are doing in their lives. I do things to send the message that I genuinely care about them and that knowing who they are is as important as running the business. I try to make communications relevant to them, not just the company. My test is at the end of the day whether they can talk to their significant others about their work in a way that makes what we are doing understandable. If so, then I know I'm on message. If you don't care about others, why should they care about the company?

David Woodward, former CEO at Heinz Europe, insists that 'You have to get on with people' and that 'If you get to the point of confrontation in a relationship, something has failed – and it's probably you!' Relationships at work are not about being best friends, though: 'I believe it's about putting respect first and then being liked. It's essential to treat people the way you want to be treated.' When he was President in the organization, he made sure he spoke to everyone in the same respectful way without strict adherence to hierarchy: 'It maybe set me apart.'

We resonated, too, with the perspective of Emma Gilthorpe, COO at Heathrow:

Having positive relationships in work is fundamental. They are a massive spur to success. For instance, creating bonds with people based on shared commitment, loyalty and discretionary effort is born out of strong relationships. On the other hand, where relationships are compromised you will fail to capitalize on capability and effort. Having negativity in relationships sucks time and energy. You end up with your brain parallel-processing what's going on.

The critical skills to build great relationships – empathy, under-standing, compassion, acceptance, openness and communication – are underpinned by emotional intelligence (EI).

This concept came to a wide awareness with the publication of *Emotional Intelligence: Why It Can Matter More Than IQ*, written by author and science journalist Daniel Goleman. A few years earlier Goleman had read an article by two professors and friends, Peter Salovey and John Mayer, sparking a eureka moment which Goleman described in this way:

> Those were days when the pre-eminence of IQ as the standard of excellence in life was unquestioned; a debate raged over whether it was set in our genes or due to experience. But here, suddenly, was a new way of thinking about the ingredients of life success. I was electrified by the notion, which I made the title of [my] book in 1995. (Goleman, 1996)

In *Emotional Intelligence*, Goleman outlined EI in four fundamental ways:

1 **Self-awareness** – the ability to understand your own emotional state at any given time and accurately see how others see you
2 **Social awareness** – the ability to take the perspective of and empathize with others from diverse backgrounds and cultures
3 **Self-management** – the ability to regulate your own emotions and control the impact of them on others
4 **Social skills** – the ability to communicate and interact with others.

The good news with EI is that whatever your current level (and it is measurable!), you can improve it.

Diana is probably one of the most emotionally intelligent people we have encountered. From humble origins, she has developed an uncanny knack of reading others, quickly attuning herself to their context, preferences and needs, which enables her to build powerful rapport and deep connections. From every direction Diana has a meaningful impact on others. She takes time to get to know her team members – their hopes, fears, successes and struggles both at work and life. She invests in developing their careers and has a track record second to none for supporting people in accelerating their work success, including promotions, showcasing work and creating opportunities.

Diana quickly establishes trust and combines a strategic focus with the ability to deliver results through others. She is welcomed as a team player, collaborating effectively with her peers, ensuring win/win outcomes and remaining egoless in her interactions. Diana is also brilliant with external stakeholders as a consequence of her thorough preparation. She makes sure to listen to understand before seeking to be understood, and adjusts her communication to the audience, which makes her accessible and engaging.

Was Diana born with this ability? No, of course not. As Daniel Goleman says:

> All these skills are learned in life. We can improve on any of them we care about, but it takes time, effort, and perseverance. It helps to have a model, someone who embodies the skill we want to improve. But we also need to practice whenever a naturally occurring opportunity arises – and it may be listening to a teenager, not just a moment at work. (Goleman, 1996)

When we asked Diana about how she developed her skillset, she was quick to point out that while at school one of her teachers encouraged her to get feedback about her strengths and weaknesses so that she could accelerate her learning. From then on Diana made a point of asking for feedback on a regular basis. Simply the act of asking others about their point of view elicited comments about her curiosity, courage, openness and honesty. This built her confidence, raised her self-awareness, helped her to manage her emotions and adapt to others. Diana is the first to admit that she has a quick temper and can easily overreact to situations, so learning to moderate her impulses has been vital to developing relationships. She also recognizes that her innate curiosity has meant that she always wants to know about others and that this has translated into acute empathy. Every couple of years Diana conducted a formal feedback process in her workplace as part of a coaching programme, getting a rounded picture from her boss, peers, direct reports and other select stakeholders. Diana made sure to include people with whom she had a spiky relationship to pick up on any of her blind spots. She has prioritized improving her EI and has benefited accordingly.

Contrast this with some examples of where we see low EI causing damage in relationships.

Paul was a 'deal maker'. We coached him at a time when he was tasked with leading a disposal programme for the major assets of his company. However, he was reliant on collaborating with others to get it done, and due to his aggressive and dominating approach the majority of people avoided him and certainly weren't disposed to helping him with open arms. Paul was in denial about the severity of the situation and potential risk to the execution of his programme, so we conducted a 360-degree feedback exercise to raise his awareness about the impact of his behaviour. The message was loud and clear. Paul failed to listen to people and consider their point of view, and appeared to simply expect others to follow his way. Thankfully, he took the feedback to heart and went back to those who had contributed to explain this learning and his commitments going forward, which included getting to know people beyond the task at hand, seeking insight about what was working and what could be improved. On completion of the project, Paul had developed a high support network across the organization and transformed his reputation from 'deal maker' to 'trusted partner'.

Tina was brilliant at delivering on big projects in complex environments. However, she created enemies along the way by coming across as controlling, manipulative and deceptive in her approach. Tina had a tendency to play people off against each other to get her own way, and if anyone dared to disagree with her, she would cut them out of the loop. Unfortunately, Tina refused to get feedback as she believed that if others couldn't deal with her, it was their problem. Eventually, even though the organization valued her work ethic and results, Tina's inability to form strong and enduring relationships proved her downfall and she was let go.

John was director of sales for a telecommunications company. He was responsible for acquiring new customers and worked at a relentless pace. As is often the case, the only way John could hit his target was in partnership with others. The trouble was that most people avoided him as they found him dismissive and arrogant. He had to have the last word in conversations and was fixated on 'being right', rather than finding the 'right way'. John's manager was an advocate of coaching and insisted that John change, or he would be changed. One of our first tasks was to conduct a 360-feedback process to ensure we were working with accurate data. The message was loud and clear. John's style alienated him from others. People did not trust him, and they worked with him only when absolutely necessary. We held up the mirror for him to reflect upon this insight. He didn't like it but recognized that there was truth in it, and became determined to change his ways. John set up one-to-one meetings with all his key stakeholders for the purpose of understanding their agendas and how he could help them succeed. This was a complete U-turn from his previous behaviour, and although he encountered some initial scepticism, over time he rebuilt relationships by consistently demonstrating higher empathy and meeting others' needs.

> Good relationships are good for business.

Research shows that EI is a better predictor of success at work than IQ. Travis Bradberry, co-author of *Emotional Intelligence 2.0* says that 'Emotional intelligence is the strongest predictor of performance', explaining a full 58% of success in all types of jobs.

He shares some fascinating results from research that he's been part of: 'Of all the people we've studied at work, we found that 90% of top performers are also high in emotional intelligence. You can be a top performer without emotional intelligence, but it's much less likely. Conversely, we discovered 20% of bottom performers are high in emotional intelligence.'

Joel Burrows, CEO at Ghirardelli, reinforced the importance of relationships:

> Most of the stuff I do involves working with others so having great relationships is critical at work. Most things get done in teams and across functions. You have to figure out how to work together including how to disagree to arrive at better outcomes. I have found that if you don't have a strong relationship it's hard to disagree. Whereas if you have a good relationship then others will understand where you are coming from, helping you to end up in a position where you can help each other.

Great relationships are a fundamental element of doing the work you love. Make them a priority. Develop your EI so that you are able to build trusting and collaborative relationships which generate win/win outcomes. Get feedback on your EI so that you can accurately self-assess how you come across and the impact you have in relationships.

For a basic quick test ask approximately eight people you work with the following questions:

1 What do you appreciate about working with me?

2 What do I do that adds the most value for you?

3 What do I do that frustrates you?

4 What can I do differently to make the biggest difference in the quality of our relationship?

Reflect on the main themes that emerge and design a plan of action to address them.

Lovenote

An increase in relationship intelligence is the smartest way to
make great work possible.

The currency of partnership

What is your approach to trust? Do you trust until proven otherwise,
or do you require evidence in order to trust? Either way, trust is the
glue that makes relationships stick, and your ability to develop strong
trust is vital for your success at work.

On one occasion we coached two people in a partnership whose
high friction was reducing the effectiveness of their work. They
described the root cause of the issue as a breakdown in trust. When
we enquired about their approach to trust, we got opposite answers.
One partner (A) had implicit trust and extended themselves fully to
others. The other partner (B) had virtually zero trust, and anyone
in their vicinity had to earn it over time by delivering on promises.
Once they had articulated their differences, we were able to help
them reset expectations for working together using a six-stage relationship model known as 'The anatomy of a relationship':

APPRECIATION

FAMILIARITY

EXPECTATIONS

DISAPPOINTMENT

GRIEVANCE

BEING RIGHT

The anatomy of a relationship

The model works in the following way:

Appreciation	At some point in a relationship there is mutual appreciation. This often occurs at the beginning (the honeymoon phase) where baggage hasn't been picked up and we show up as our best selves.
Familiarity	After a period of time familiarity creeps in as the novelty wears off and we start reacting to the things that don't work for us and accumulating baggage.
Expectations	People have expectations in relationships, most of which are not communicated and therefore not met. For instance, we expect others to understand, communicate and behave in ways that they are unaware of and therefore we set ourselves up for disappointment.
Disappointment	Once expectations have not been met, we land up frustrated and start collecting reasons to be resentful.
Grievance	This unhealthy place in a relationship is caused by unresolved issues and unspoken frustrations, leading to emotional baggage which weighs a relationship down and can cause toxicity to set in.
Being right	This is at the bottom of a relationship curve where we interpret others' behaviour in ways that fit our beliefs about how they are. At this point we go out to seek evidence to prove that we are right and to reinforce our point of view.

However difficult a relationship, there is the potential for us to work our way back up to a place of appreciation. The critical ingredient is setting and managing expectations. To return to the dysfunctional partnership we mentioned above, we asked both parties to express their expectations for working together. Partner A shared that she expected:

- to be trusted, given autonomy and freedom within a framework
- to have direct, open and honest communication
- to be valued for contributing great work.

This contrasted with partner B's expectations:

- to be updated on work plans with frequent detailed briefs
- for partner A to meet her own needs without proactive communication
- for partner A to deliver as part of the job.

You can see how different expectations of this kind can lead to different realities, which can lead to a breakdown in a relationship. In this instance we had both partner A and B summarize each other's expectations to check for understanding. We then asked them to explain how these expectations could be met from a behavioural perspective. Partner A proposed the following:

- Once they had agreed on a plan, she would be allowed to get on with it, reaching out to B only if there were any issues to resolve.
- She would give feedback in real time on what was working/not working.
- They would share, recognize and celebrate success together.

Partner B proposed the following:

- There should be a daily check-in to progress work and a weekly one-page report to give a detailed outline.
- Each should focus on their personal agenda without needing to check in with the other.
- They would complete tasks and move on.

Once we had the specifics on the table, they were able to see how far apart they were in terms of managing their expectations. This heightened awareness enabled them to de-personalize the situation and see that without understanding each other's expectations, they could not be in a position to meet them. We were then able to help the parties agree a contract for working together to set them up for success. This included the following:

- Make no assumptions – listen to understand.
- Take responsibility – meet your own needs.
- Have each other's back – ask for help.

> Setting clear expectations builds trust.

We are great believers in establishing short and simple working contracts both in individual and team relationships to build the trust factor. These contracts set expectations and provide a common language to use. They also provide a practical way of evidencing trust as everyone has a nuanced interpretation of what trust means.

Khaled Ismail, Vice President Communications, Europe, Central Asia, Middle East and Africa, Tetra Pak, reminded us of another vital ingredient for trust – empathy:

This is where you genuinely put yourself in other people's shoes. For instance, during the COVID-19 pandemic it has meant truly understanding the reality of someone living in an apartment with two children when they are supposed to work from home in an effective way. It means listening to challenges rather than trying to counter arguments and extending active listening rather than preparing your responses. From a leadership perspective, empathy means leading by example – for instance ensuring that you don't tell others to do things that you wouldn't do. It is essential to walk the talk and engage with people as normal human beings.

An example of establishing a team contract to help manage trust was when we worked with a commercial leadership team. The team consisted of a mix of backgrounds, personalities and capabilities which, when blended together, presented challenges in the way members communicated, collaborated and got stuff done. However, the main issue they talked about in our diagnostic interviews was about a lack of trust. It was almost as if they questioned each other's intent and found it difficult to take things at face value, as if they believed that there were hidden agendas at play. On surfacing these issues, we addressed the team collectively and challenged them to agree a team contract. After considerable debate they alighted on the following:

- **Assume good intent** – give people the benefit of the doubt.
- **Go direct** – be brave and communicate directly with people rather than going behind their backs.
- **Let go** – be prepared to drop any misconceptions.

These behavioural indicators gave the team a framework within which they could work together and start the process of rebuilding trust.

In a 2017 *Harvard Business Review* article, 'The neuroscience of trust', Paul J. Zak explains why trust is so important in a team or company and grounds this firmly in science:

> Employees in high-trust organizations are more productive, have more energy at work, collaborate better with their colleagues, and stay with their employers longer than people working at low-trust companies. They also suffer less chronic stress and are happier with their lives, and these factors fuel stronger performance. (Zak, 2017)

In his study Zak and his team sought to measure trust and reciprocation (trustworthiness) by calibrating the oxytocin levels of participants. Oxytocin is a hormone produced by the hypothalamus – a small region at the base of our brain – which has a positive impact on social behaviours related to trust, relaxation and overall psychological stability. Their research showed that oxytocin increases a person's empathy, a useful trait for social creatures trying to work together.

Zak identified eight management behaviours that foster trust. The most relevant one for this chapter is to 'intentionally build relationships'. He writes:

The brain network that oxytocin activates is evolutionarily old. This means that the trust and sociality that oxytocin enables are deeply embedded in our nature. Yet at work we often get the message that we should focus on completing tasks, not on making friends. Neuroscience experiments by my lab show that when people intentionally build social ties at work, their performance improves. A Google study similarly found that managers who 'express interest in and concern for team members' success and personal well-being' outperform others in the quality and quantity of their work. (Zak, 2017)

Emma Gilthorpe, COO at Heathrow, invests heavily in creating environments of trust:

To create a positive relationship based on trust you need to find what gets people buzzing. For instance, at Heathrow when we were looking at building a third runway, I found that it was essential to understand what people cared about on a personal level and tap into it. Some people were excited about the engineering challenge, whereas others cared passionately about creating a brilliant community impact. It's vital to spend time investing in relationships so that you can make a difference by understanding what makes others tick.

Likewise, Laura Miller, Executive Vice President, Chief Information Officer, at Macy's, emphasized the need for building trust:

I noticed that during COVID-19 we were almost starving for the relationship element of work. It is what nurtures our soul. People want connections, and they love it when connections are meaningful and yield trust. For instance, some of my best friends have come from work relationships. I used to keep work and relationships separate. However, I came to realize that work is such an immersive experience that I need the personal relationships at work to keep connected, and trust was at the heart of them.

How do you go about cultivating trust at work? Are you known for building high-trust relationships and environments where others thrive, or do you inadvertently cause people to walk on eggshells around you because they don't know whether they can trust you? Our experience shows that those people who do foster trust create loyalty and stickiness in their relationships, which adds a whole other dimension to work.

A simple exercise to conduct is to write down three ways that you believe you build trust and three ways that you think you either break trust or could break trust. Examples might include:

Trust builders

... display humility and vulnerability	... are approachable and share freely
... create psychological safety	... are present and pay attention
... have deep empathy and compassion	... are sincere and genuinely care for others
... lead with purpose and passion	... encourage different points of view and debate
... have an inspirational presence	... are consistently reliable
... are fun to be around	... possess a high degree of technical capability

Trust breakers

... are arrogant or egotistical	... are distracted and too busy for others
... seek own celebrity	... stifle debate and reject different points of view
... blame others instead of taking personal responsibility	... act as a disciplinarian or dictator
... exhibit dishonesty or insincerity	... seek to control, instead of developing, others
... are unreliable and cannot be counted on to keep a commitment	... fail to deliver what is promised
... are detached or unapproachable	... have no tolerance for mistakes

Once you have completed your own self-reflection, we suggest that you get feedback from various people to test your own view. It's vital to be aware of the impact you have and whether you stimulate the release of oxytocin in others or not. Start from a place of trusting others until proven otherwise. Be clear about how you can demonstrate your trust and instigate transparent conversations with people you work with about how to get the best out of one another.

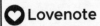 **Lovenote**

Take yourself to the edge of transparency in your relationships to close any trust gaps.

Inclusion

On 25 May 2020, Minneapolis police officers arrested George Floyd, a 46-year-old black man, after a convenience store employee called 911 and told the police that Mr Floyd had bought cigarettes with a counterfeit $20 bill. Seventeen minutes after the first squad car arrived at the scene, George Floyd was unconscious and pinned beneath three police officers, showing no signs of life. A lawyer acting for George Floyd's family told a memorial service that a 'pandemic of racism' had led to his death. George Floyd's killing, which was captured on video, caused outrage and sparked a wave of protests in cities across the US and beyond.

George Floyd's tragic death was a stark reminder that all of us need to truly understand and respond to diversity and inclusion. In our work, it has led to a high demand from clients wanting to engage in meaningful conversations in this area. However, there has also been an accompanying fear factor about giving people voice and sharing views. We believe it's essential to be informed and raise awareness about what diversity and inclusion means and how to embrace it in a work environment so that you can operate with heightened sensitivity.

So what is diversity?

Philip was selected as high-potential talent in his organization. He was fast-tracked for promotion when we were asked to coach him as preparation for a senior role interview. Philip came across as thoughtful and confident when discussing his background, capability and future ambition. However, when we asked him to consider any potential roadblocks that he might encounter as part of his progression, he retreated within himself and went quiet. After a lengthy pause Philip said he was going to disclose something he had never told anyone in the workplace – his sexuality. Philip was gay and was afraid that if this information surfaced, he could experience discrimination and reach a glass ceiling. We checked whether he had any evidence to support his fear, and he cited how he had overheard some biased remarks from colleagues about the LGBTQ community. We suggested that he discuss his concern with the HR Director whom we trusted implicitly. Rightly, she was very supportive of Philip and concerned about his comments. She gave him the assurance that if he did experience any discrimination, he was to inform her immediately and that she would take the appropriate action. Thankfully, this alleviated his concerns, and he went on to secure the role. Philip went from strength to strength, and one year later he became the Chair for the company's LGBTQ group and started to educate people across the organization about the importance of diversity and inclusion.

Diversity is any dimension that can be used to differentiate groups and people from one another – respecting and appreciating what makes us different. Some elements of diversity are visible such as gender, language, age, ethnicity and some disabilities. However, the majority of what makes us different is unseen including physical ability, sexual orientation, gender identity, marital status, thinking style, income level, skills, religion, political preference, job level, education, family status, culture, values, experience and invisible disabilities. What we notice in the workplace is that it's rare to come across environments where people are encouraged to discuss the invisible aspects of diversity or made to feel comfortable about them.

On one occasion we were coaching a leadership team which wanted to strengthen its connectivity. The team had worked together for the best part of three years; however, their interactions were primarily task-focused. We orchestrated an exercise where each team member had the opportunity to share a personal story designed to disclose the unseen aspects of themselves. They were asked to select several experiences which would give the team valuable insight. People were apprehensive; the CEO, in particular, was uncomfortable about what might happen. To manage expectations we suggested that each person would have 15 minutes to share their story. With ten members on the team this should have been a two-and-a-half-hour exercise forming part of an all-day agenda. However, seven hours later the team were still sharing stories. People were immersed in understanding each other's histories, which gave them new perspectives on their differences and deepened their appreciation of one another. The CEO warmed to the process and gave us licence to keep going. It became a turning point for the team in their respect and appreciation of what made each member different.

What is inclusion? Sam was known for consciously creating diverse working environments. The team he formed possessed a healthy mix of different genders, ethnicities, personalities, ages, experiences and capabilities. He also ensured that everyone was encouraged to work in collaborative and transparent ways − sharing information freely, focusing on improving things together and being given equal opportunities to thrive. Sam invited us to coach the team to maximize its potential. Our starting point was to gather insight from team members about what was working and what could be improved. Some gaps began to emerge. People talked about the sense that there was an 'in' and 'out' group within the team where some appeared to be more included than others. Some felt that Sam had a couple of go-to people who always seemed to cover for him and had the opportunity to gain visibility with senior leadership. People struggled with the different personalities in the team, as some members came across as loud and forceful in their views, dominating conversations and showing low sensitivity to others. Some described how there seemed to be an 'entitlement culture' where those with long service appeared to expect preferential treatment.

When we shared these findings with Sam, he was grateful for the perspective and slightly dismayed that, while he had tried so hard to create a diverse mix on his team, there were still examples of exclusion being evidenced.

We gave him other examples of exclusion we had observed else-where including:

- White men in organizations that prioritized ethnic minorities, women and members of LGBTQ communities felt ostracized by the company and were concerned that they would get left on a 'scrap heap'.
- Women felt they were products of positive discrimination when going for jobs, as if filling a female quota in the company was more important than seeking the right person for the role.

We told him that we often encountered situations where, although there might be *visible* signs of diversity, a truly inclusive environment nonetheless did not exist, and issues inevitably arose. We put forward our definition of inclusion: the creation of an environment where groups or individuals with different backgrounds are culturally and socially accepted, welcomed, treated equally and have voice.

We agreed with Sam to start a development journey with the team focused on creating an inclusive culture. We brought the team together, shared members' insights, and ensured that we had the right psycho-logical safety for everyone to have voice and contribute points of view without fearing any negative consequences. We helped raise awareness about topics like diversity, inclusion, bias (conscious and unconscious), and the key moments of choice as a team where they could truly demonstrate inclusive behaviour such as working with people who are not like them, running team and project meetings, and acting when they see or hear exclusion. We brought in dimensions such as team pur-pose, values, vision, strengths and ways of working to broaden perspec-tives and provide different filters for creating an inclusive environment.

We asked the team about times in their work when they felt excluded and the impact it had. Examples included:

- The marketing director who had often been criticized for poor spelling in written communication. It wasn't until they were diagnosed as dyslexic at the age of 40 that they could appreciate their own profile and explain it to others.

- The operational director who felt left out of 'strategic' conversations as if their point of view was not as valid as their 'corporate' colleagues who were more familiar dealing with glossy PowerPoint decks.
- The people director who cited examples of when they were not invited to performance meetings as if the people element was not important in driving results.
- A long-serving black member of the team who felt that they had reached a glass ceiling in their career and that the company didn't value who they were and what they had to offer.
- An introverted and quiet team member who felt that they got overlooked in meetings because they weren't as skilled at speaking up quickly and loudly.

We then asked them to share examples from their life to show exclusion at play in other environments. They shared the following:

- A colleague who had been a talented sportsperson whose sporting dreams had ended after a severe bullying episode in which he was assaulted and had a leg broken.
- A colleague who had German Jewish heritage and who experienced anti-Semitism growing up in the UK.
- A colleague who had been called 'stupid' by a teacher at school and developed an 'imposter syndrome' complex, feeling 'less than' in both social and work situations.
- A colleague who had a visual impairment and got left out of sporting activities at school.
- A colleague who was childless as a result of being unable to conceive who felt left out when conversations turned to family life.

Having these conversations challenged team members to reflect upon their bias – conscious and unconscious. It's vital to understand bias because it's part of the human condition. It is our belief that, while it's difficult to eliminate bias, we can learn to outsmart our own biases.

Bias is an inclination or prejudice for or against one person, or group, or thing. Unconscious (or implicit) bias refers to a bias that we are unaware of and which happens outside our control. It is a bias that happens automatically and is triggered by our brain making quick judgements and assessments of people and situations, influenced by our background, cultural environment and personal experiences. There are now divided opinions on whether training against it can be enough to remove the problem, but an awareness of its existence can help with our empathy and approach to inclusion.

In *Thinking, Fast and Slow* (2011), Nobel Memorial Prize in Economic Sciences laureate Daniel Kahneman suggests there are two modes of thought: 'System 1' is fast, instinctive and emotional; 'System 2' is slower, more deliberate and more logical. Kahneman challenges us to consider that although System 1 is critical for survival – making us swerve to avoid a car, for example – it is also a common source of bias that can result in poor decision making. This perspective is reinforced from the work of neuroscientists who estimate that the human body sends 11 million bits of information per second to the brain for processing, yet the conscious mind seems to be able to process only 50 bits per second. The unconscious mind, operating on autopilot, manages the rest. As a result the brain creates mental shortcuts to help us interpret information faster and save energy in decision making.

Back to the team. Creating the conditions where people could speak up about experiences of exclusion and normalizing bias as part of the human condition opened the door to greater honesty and courage in facing the immediate issues within the team. We set up a feedback exercise where people were invited to have individual conversations with team members to share perceptions of when they felt excluded or included in the relationship and the impact that it had. We encouraged the team to use and complete the following statements:

A time I felt included in our relationship was ...

A time I felt excluded in our relationship was ...

People needed to listen to the statements and could respond only by saying 'thank you' and not give defensive responses or justifications. By the time people had received statements from all team members, there were some consistent themes emerging, which helped individuals to feel they were not under personal attack. This structure enabled team members to share unspoken experiences, bringing immediate relief and, in some cases, helping to clear the air.

We reconvened as a team and listened to the insights people gleaned from going through the exercise. Although the majority of participants found it uncomfortable (most forms of learning and development are stretching), there was sincere appreciation of the process. We asked people to reflect upon any pattern or theme, linked to an instance where they had excluded or included others, and to share it with the team. It was refreshing to hear people owning their behaviour by relating how, for instance, they had excluded others by talking over them, drawing on the same people for projects, failing to allow everyone a voice in meetings, and socializing only with those who had similar interests. Examples of being inclusive included: deliberately choosing to involve people with different thinking styles on projects and giving them the licence to challenge the norm; ensuring those who needed time to reflect were given notice before important meetings to prepare their thinking; and sharing resources in selfless ways so as to prioritize the collective agenda.

Sam found it an enlightening exercise. He shared with the team his biggest learning that going out and recruiting a diverse team does not automatically lead to an inclusive environment. He realized that together they needed to create the conditions where diversity could thrive, and where everyone could have a sense of belonging. Going forward the team agreed to an approach to sustain inclusion based on three conditions:

1 **Say** – making a more inclusive culture a collective priority.
2 **Do** – ensuring that each inclusive statement is backed up with tangible action.
3 **Drive** – reinforcing opportunities to build a more inclusive culture.

As they progressed, some of the examples that were implemented included:

- holding listening forums on a regular basis to maintain a pulse check on diversity and inclusion progress and challenges
- ensuring leaders had a positive attitude towards failure and advocated a genuine learning environment
- colleagues being able to decline a request to work early or late without negative consequences
- actively encouraging virtual and remote working, making sure it was widely available and common practice
- making personal and professional development an organizational priority so that everyone felt they had the opportunity to progress
- colleagues adopting their own dress code, rather than conforming to a company norm.

We recognize that at the heart of inclusion is the opportunity for everyone to be their authentic selves at work and to belong. Appreciating difference and bringing different perspectives ensures that everyone challenges their normal ways of doing things and brings more depth to the capability of the organization and helps sustain its future.

One organization that has placed a high emphasis on creating an inclusive culture is Heathrow Airport. As the UK's biggest employment site Heathrow embraces every dimension of diversity through its engagement with colleagues, passengers and multiple stakeholder networks. In our interview with Paula Stannett, Chief People Officer, she shared how the company has created an overriding culture that values the business case for inclusion:

> We really dial up on people understanding the Heathrow way. We recognize that at the heart of inclusion is the opportunity for everyone to be their authentic selves at work and to belong. Appreciating difference and bringing different perspectives ensures that everyone challenges their normal ways of doing things and brings more depth to the capability of the organization and helps sustain its future.

She argues that 'inclusion is bigger than diversity'. While, in an organizational context, diversity often focuses on achieving targets (e.g. gender, ethnicity, age and disability), inclusion is about 'the systemic culture of an organization including its purpose, vision, values, leadership, behaviours and strategic choices'. At Heathrow, she says, 'We focus on being a great place to work where everyone can come to work as their true selves and reach their potential.'

Another company that prioritizes an inclusive culture is The Standard Hotels. Amar Lalvani, CEO of parent group Standard International, shared what it means from his perspective: 'Elimination of rigid thinking within the organization, breaking down hierarchy, not allowing anyone especially senior leaders to take themselves too seriously and cultivating intense curiosity and passion for shareable discoveries.' However, he recognizes that the work is never completed and remains an ongoing priority.

We believe that companies which are deliberate in creating inclusive environments become magnets for amazing people who want to do amazing work. Be one of them. Challenge yourself to define what diversity and inclusion mean to you and how you can demonstrate a genuine awareness and approach to becoming more diverse and inclusive. Recognize that bias is a natural condition. You will never rid yourself of bias. However, continuing to increase your awareness of bias and the impact it has will help you get the right mix of 'Say, Do and Drive' so you can back up your intent with action.

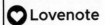 **Lovenote**

Be you. Let others be who they are.

Sharing the story

Tell me a story. Four simple words that evoke memories, emotions and curiosity. Humans are natural storytellers. Given the amount of data we are exposed to through emails, instant messaging, documentation, conference calls, newspapers, social networking sites … the list goes on … our brains are constantly having to work out what is useful and necessary and what it can let go of. Stories are the best way to simplify complexity and to make points stick.

Psychologists at McMaster University in Hamilton, Ontario, are exploring the mechanisms deep within the brain to better understand just what happens when we communicate. New research published in the *Journal of Cognitive Neuroscience* (Brown et al., 2018) suggests that no matter how a narrative is expressed – through words, gestures or drawings – our brains relate best to the characters, focusing on the thoughts and feelings of the protagonist of each story.

We were fortunate to work with Janet who was an extraordinary storyteller and CEO of a global company. On one occasion we were facilitating a leadership development programme for one of her customer groups. She was scheduled to open the event with a 60-minute slot sharing her perspective on leadership and the lessons she had learned along her path to becoming a CEO. Two hours later we were still immersed in her stories, which took us on a journey from her childhood, introducing us to the characters who had shaped her values and influenced her philosophy as a leader to those in her current-day environment.

Janet grew up in a difficult family context. Her father was an alcoholic, and the family lived on eggshells trying to anticipate his mood and manage the consequences of his drinking. Her mother was in constant denial: she defended her husband and made excuses for his addiction, putting it down to the pressure of work and his needing an outlet. Janet had a younger sister who had a disability. Her parents struggled to adjust to the level of care required, so Janet often had to step in to perform tasks beyond her years. Janet was extremely bright at school; however, her parents were not able to embrace the sharpness of her intellect and simply let her get on with it. Her background led to the development of strong values such as independence, autonomy, caring for others and accountability.

As a consequence of these experiences, Janet developed a leadership philosophy which came straight from her heart and included the following ideas:

- **Leadership is not a title.** Janet believed passionately that everyone is a leader and with the right attitude can develop

the initiative, insight and skills to create followership and
deliver results.

- **Everyone deserves a chance.** Given her background,
  Janet was passionate about ensuring everyone had equal
  opportunities to excel and believed that all human
  potential could be developed.
- **Learn from those you serve.** Janet was attuned to
  her multiple stakeholder groups including colleagues,
  customers, consumers, community and shareholders. She
  invested considerable time in understanding their needs
  and actively sought feedback, which she then acted on to
  improve the business.

In our session we moved into a Q&A where no questions were
out of bounds. The customer group wanted to know more about her
background, lessons learned and how she continued to show up and be
on top of her game while juggling her relentless schedule. Janet shared
how one of her mentors had helped her learn how to be present and
available as a leader. One idea the mentor talked about was the 'leader's
walk' – how when leaders walk through an office it should be a chance
to connect with people rather than just a matter of getting from A to
B. She shared how the leader is the 'weather' – in other words, how, as
a leader, your mood is infectious – and that therefore you need to be
very deliberate about what you are spreading. She talked, too, about the
'elevator moment': when you are in a lift, don't just look at the floor –
engage; talk with people; use humour to break the ice.

Janet made it personal by talking about the challenges she faced
being a mother. She talked about 'carpet time': when her children
were younger, on returning home, she would straightaway get on
the floor to be at the same level as them and play with them before
embarking on any other tasks. She had a close-knit group of friends
with whom she would play tennis every week so she could mix having fun with exercise.

> Stories make connections.

How effective is your storytelling? When you focus on building relationships, how much consideration do you give to the power of stories? Have you taken the time to craft a series of stories that give you the intended impact and influence you seek? We have been on a learning journey in our own work by becoming better story-tellers. On one occasion we were running a coaching development programme for an entertainment company that prided itself on sto-rytelling. We were taking quite a purist approach to coaching, mainly focusing on the technical skills of a coach, until one brave participant gave us feedback that they wanted more stories about the people we coached so that they could learn from real scenarios. This opened a door for us to bring more of who we were to the programme based on stories. Since then the majority of the principles and practices we teach are grounded in stories to made them accessible and memorable.

What is the compelling and memorable story about your work that engages and inspires? It is essential to develop this whether you want to get people to buy into your current work offer, or you are looking at creating your next work opportunity, for instance through an inter-view. We suggest using the following principles to guide your story.

1. Have a clear and compelling message

What is the memorable headline that will catch attention? If you look at political campaigns, they often feature a simple slogan that drives a message home to voters. Setting aside whatever political beliefs we have, we can all recognize the power of the British Conservative Party drumming home 'Get Brexit done' in the 2019 UK parliamen-tary elections, or of Donald Trump's message 'Make America great again' in his successful 2016 presidential campaign.

Jonathan Coen, Security Director at Heathrow, talked to us about his need to create a compelling message to engage over 4,000 col-leagues early on in his tenure:

On a personal level, inspiration is what makes my blood rush. This happens when I get an emotional connection with the task in hand and the picture being painted. When I came into the Security role, I was challenged by John Holland-Kaye, my CEO, who asked me, 'How could I create a new industry standard?' This took me on a journey to try something new and to create change for the better. I established a message based on three core ideas – 'Protect, Serve and Grow'. Simply put, the Security function exists to protect the nation. We serve thousands of passengers every day, and our success helps to unlock the growth of the company. The team connected with the message, raised their game and it drove momentum.

In a different context we coached a COO in the health sector. Jo was looking at expanding her career and needed to create a compelling message for interviews. She had been advised by an experienced head-hunter to prepare a memorable story lasting about two minutes to demonstrate where she had come from, where she was now and where she was going. We challenged Jo to define three things that she wanted to make memorable and leave as an impression on others. She recognized that her core strengths were being people-oriented, influencing senior stakeholders in complex and political environments, and delivering commercial results. She drilled these down to her fundamental message:

1 Lead with compassion.
2 Get buy-in.
3 Make change happen.

She found this an extremely useful anchor in her interviews, and the feedback she got from the head-hunter was that she came across with clarity, focus and energy, which quickly enabled her to get a bigger and better role.

2. Evidence with examples and key data

Our second principle is to back up each message with a memorable example and/or data. In Jonathan Coen's message, as shared above, he evidenced what 'protecting the nation' meant in terms of tangible metrics as well as giving examples about the amazing work security officers do to keep the nation safe. He did the same for 'serve and grow' to win hearts and minds. The COO in the health sector demonstrated how she led with compassion, drawing on a story of how she led the transformation of an organization by driving efficiencies while enabling colleagues to adapt and upgrade their roles. To evidence her ability to get buy-in she shared a story about influencing government to change industry regulation (for which she was awarded a CBE). To show her ability to make change happen she shared the financial results in a role where she had reduced costs and increased revenue.

It's important to remember that everyone has different preferences on how they like to hear evidence. For some, there still needs to be an emotional connection, in which case real-life stories work well. For others, sharing numbers is what is required.

3. Share the ask

It's important to be clear and upfront about what you want from others. For instance, if you are seeking a role, telling others about what would make your heart sing will enable them to know whether they are in a position to help you. If you are in a role where you want to create change, it's vital to ask for this clearly in order to see whether it's realistic.

Although being clear about what you are asking is often uncomfortable, it's possible to do so in an engaging and sensitive way where you can show your empathy and awareness of others, rather than coming across as only motivated by selfish wants. Robin had been in a business partnership for over 20 years. He had successfully co-created a business which had put him in a position of financial freedom. His partner was still highly driven to grow the business and increase revenue, whereas Robin had reached a point where he was motivated to help influence the future direction of the company. However, he was no longer prepared to work all hours and run the day-to-day operation. We coached Robin on how he would ask his business partner for what he wanted going forward – more influence, less management, more space, fewer hours. Robin set the context with his partner and shared his ask. To his surprise, the partner responded in a very positive way, acknowledged that they wanted different things (his partner wanted to continue driving the business day to day), but he massively valued Robin's contribution and they agreed to find a way forward.

4. Understand the benefits

It is vital to finish a story with 'what's in it for them' so that you find the mutual benefit. In the example above, Robin's partner shared that if he went on to grow the company value and increase revenue without Robin involved, it would be a hollow victory. The act of doing it together was as important for him as making money. With this understanding in place, Robin was able to pledge his commitment so that they both benefited from the outcome. It's essential to seek to understand the potential benefits for others in any proposition you are putting forward. Once you have this information, you are in a position to see what's possible. We often find that people become too focused on their own agenda rather than showing the necessary awareness and appreciation of others.

> ### ♥ Lovenote
>
> Humans buy emotionally and then justify rationally. Stories with substance help people buy into you.

At the heart of it

To thrive at work, it is vital to invest smartly in your relationships.

Your emotional 'bank accounts' with others need continuous, skilled management.

Exchange the five types of relationship currency to develop a healthy balance:

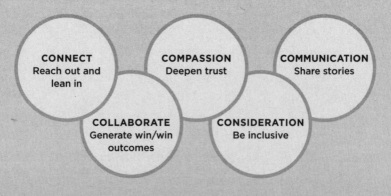

CONNECT
Reach out and lean in

COMPASSION
Deepen trust

COMMUNICATION
Share stories

COLLABORATE
Generate win/win outcomes

CONSIDERATION
Be inclusive

6

Accelerate evolution

The art of embracing change

In a 2020 *Time* article titled 'Superforecasters are making eerily accurate predictions about COVID-19: Our leaders could learn from their approach', health and science reporter Tara Law drew our attention to a different way of anticipating the future as pioneered by Good Judgment, Inc. and the organization it spun off from, the research initiative Good Judgment Project. 'Unlike history's prophets,' Law writes, 'forecasters do not claim to possess supernatural abilities.' Instead, they say their accuracy is a result of using specific techniques to structure their thinking and constantly trying to improve their skills. Superforecasters also tend to share certain personality traits, including humility, reflectiveness and being comfortable with numbers. These characteristics might mean that they're better at putting their ego aside and are willing to change their minds when challenged with new data or ideas.

How do you go about embracing change? How do you forecast the future? How equipped are you for the continued unprecedented levels of change we are now experiencing? How good are you at putting your ego aside to explore new data or ideas? In our interview with David Woodward, former CEO Heinz Europe, he shared some personal reflections which he offered to people that he was mentoring during the early stages of the COVID-19 pandemic:

When I was leading Heinz UK and Ireland back in 2008 during the financial crisis, I thought that it couldn't get any more difficult as a leader … I was very clearly wrong! I remember feeling huge trepidation and some real fear. I was stretched massively physically and mentally. At the same time I was up for a challenge and in some ways excited about an opportunity to drive change. What we face now is much more concerning and complex, without doubt. I suggest nine things to consider:

1. We are experiencing leadership challenges tougher than many will have faced in their lifetimes. These lessons can't be taught at university or business schools, but they will make you stronger. If you can find time, keep a simple journal on a daily basis about what you have faced, how you felt and what you did … I promise you'll refer to it again later in your lives.

2. These times will bring out the very best and worst of people and leaders. For those with teams, you will find some hidden gems who come to the fore and you will probably find some empty suits. Try to not judge others too quickly but nurture and support them. Recognize you will have many people needing your leadership now more than ever.

3. Be realistic, don't sugar-coat the reality, but be upbeat and positive.

4. There will be light at the end of the tunnel … eventually.

5. The world will be different from what we've known in the past, possibly better, and now is our chance to help shape it. Think of the ways that you can rapidly drive some of the changes that you believe are required and engage others with your ideas. For instance, if one of your customer segments is decimated and likely to never return fully, then reorient towards those areas that may come through even stronger. You will have to think strategically and quickly.

6. The most adaptable and flexible will survive and thrive … inertia must be avoided.

7. Given that many people are working at home, use it as a time to connect more deeply with your families and friends.

8. Communicate, communicate and communicate ... You cannot overdo it, whether it's a few minutes on the phone, social media apps or structured conference calls. People need to feel fully engaged, challenged, understood and appreciated. Listen more carefully than you talk, because it is essential that people can unburden emotionally. Two ears and one mouth, right?

9. Look after yourself. Eat well, take exercise, limit the amount of news you watch and find reasons to smile!

In general, we find that there are three different personas when it comes to change:

- The Champions: 10 per cent love it – they drive change hard and thrive on the uncertainty and ambiguity;
- The Resisters: 10 per cent resist it – they avoid change, deny its existence and live on the nostalgia of the past;
- The Adopters: 80 per cent wait – they don't lead change and they don't block it, but they need to be taken on an intellectual and emotional journey to embrace change.

A useful reminder for relating to the impact of change over time is recognizing the four stages we can encounter:

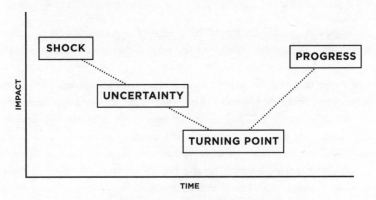

The impact of change over time

Let's use the COVID-19 pandemic as one example. Our initial response to the pandemic – and the change it swiftly brought about – was **shock**, especially when compounded by such media headlines as:

Growing fear you can catch Covid-19 more than once as patients who've recovered start to test positive again

Daily Mail, 14 April 2020

CORONAVIRUS. HOW SCARED SHOULD WE BE?

Coronavirus has been described as an invisible killer. What could be more terrifying than that?

BBC News, 24 May 2020

COVID-19'S SCARY BLOOD CLOTS AREN'T THAT SURPRISING

There's more than a century of research linking clogged blood vessels to infectious diseases

Wired, 5 July 2020

Shock is usually triggered by a lack of information, fear of the unknown, feeling threatened, or the fear of doing something wrong. It can lead to a state of paralysis where people wait to find out how real is the fear and the potential implications. This activates the next stage – **uncertainty**. If you're like most people, uncertainty can cause tremendous anxiety. Why? Your survival brain is constantly updating your world, making judgements about what's safe and what isn't. Due to its dislike of uncertainty, the brain makes up all sorts of untested stories because, to the brain, uncertainty equals danger. If your brain doesn't know what's around the corner, it can't keep you out of harm's way. It always assumes the worst, over-personalizes threats and jumps to conclusions. (Your brain will do almost anything for the sake of certainty.) You're hard-wired to overestimate threats and underestimate your ability to handle them – all in the name of survival.

When certainty is questioned, your stress response goes haywire, instantly arousing your fight-or-flight reaction, in an attempt to spur you into action and get you to safety. Waiting for certainty can feel like torture by a million tiny cuts. Sometimes the brain prefers to know an outcome one way or another so that the edge is taken off. Studies show that you're calmer anticipating pain than anticipating uncertainty because pain is certain. Scientists have found that job uncertainty, for example, takes a greater toll on your health than actually losing the job.

As uncertainty builds it can trigger feelings of anger, frustration and suspicion. At the peak of uncertainty, depression can set in as the impact of the actual change or threat of change is acknowledged. This phase can be associated with apathy, isolation and a sense of remoteness. It's essential at this stage to recognize that you are not alone and to have the reassurance that others are experiencing similar feelings. This helps you to develop a more stable platform and signals the **turning point** when you can begin to perceive change as opportunity.

Progress is made when optimism kicks in and change is accepted as inevitable. Early thoughts of new opportunities, relief that the change has been endured and impatience for the change to end mean that there is greater acceptance, hope and trust in the process.

It is too early to predict the full extent of the progress that may arise out of the COVID-19 pandemic. However, in our thoughts about what we call 'dynamic working' (covered in detail later in this chapter), we have looked at how people are working in different ways, accelerating changes for the better which would not have come about unless triggered by something of the magnitude of a global pandemic.

> Adopt a change mindset.

Reaching a point where you can love change is a stretch but one that we highly recommend you make. It's helpful to recognize the change that you can control, the change that you can influence and the change that is out of your hands. Staying with COVID-19 as an example, we can say that some of the changes within your control include:

- following government guidelines
- going outside and managing yourself with social distancing
- washing your hands
- eating healthily every day
- exercising daily
- performing acts of service for your family and community.

Focusing on what you *can* do is empowering and prevents you from feeling a victim of the change. Things that you could influence include:

- managing your home and work environment
- as required, supporting your children's schooling at home
- encouraging the health and wellbeing of your loved ones
- advocating for work and community initiatives
- sharing data and information in responsible ways.

The things lying outside your control include:

- the duration of the virus
- the global spread
- the impact on the economy
- travel restrictions.

Change is inevitable. Whether you're in a great work situation or a difficult one, things will change. Nothing stays the same. Many people remain unsure about their work situations, but by conducting a situational analysis – looking at what they can change, what they can't change and what they can influence – and by taking into account the impact of the change curve, they will be able to adopt a change mindset and move forward with courage and conviction.

Ahmad was positioned as the next CEO for a global company. The process had been going on for 18 months and, impatient by nature, he was keen to get resolution one way or another. We had been coaching him through the process. However, as it dragged into a new calendar year, Ahmad was on the verge of stepping out of the ring because he was now finding that the uncertainty was distracting him from his current role. We encouraged him to look at the change through the three lenses outlined above: control, influence and letting go. He recognized that he had already completed the majority of his influencing activity through multiple interviews, presentations and stakeholder meetings. He could see that the final decision was out of his hands as the board were juggling multiple data points taking into account all stakeholders. Ahmad stepped back and decided to take control of his mindset and emotions. He decided to use the experience as a learning opportunity and that, whatever the outcome, he would come out a stronger and better version of himself. Within weeks he got called up by the board to be informed that they were now accelerating the transition as the existing CEO had brought forward his retirement and he had two months to prepare. Thankfully, Ahmad was in the right place to adapt and move forward at pace.

In another example of how to manage change, Marlon had stepped into an interim role at an executive level following a surprise departure by his predecessor. It was his dream role and for the next six months he excelled at delivering on the existing strategy, planning the future and developing the team along the way. One evening we got an unexpected call from Marlon. He was in an agitated state: he had been asked to meet with the CEO who informed him in a brief five-minute meeting that he was not getting the role on a permanent basis and that his replacement would be taking over within days. Marlon was in shock. His immediate reaction was to resign. We listened to his anger and disbelief. The announcement had come out of the blue, and he wasn't prepared. He had a choice: stay or go. Staying meant taking a good hard look in the mirror, eating humble pie, and seeing it as a big learning opportunity to show himself and the organization how he could be relied upon in the face of a setback. Marlon reinvented himself. He moved into a different part of the business to acquire broader experience, supported his successor with a seamless transition, and strengthened his reputation for being an open, collaborative team player.

Tanya derived energy from driving growth in companies. She loved creating amazing customer experiences that opened new doors for innovation. When the financial crisis hit in 2008, her organization went into severe cost-cutting measures. Tanya felt out of her depth. She was unsure about how to continue driving value in a restricted environment. She brought her team together, and collectively they started working in new and collaborative ways with colleagues in the business to seek alternative options for engaging with customers in financially tight times. This experience provided a deep learning experience which gave Tanya a different mindset and skillset for dealing with change.

When the unprecedented crisis of COVID-19 happened, Tanya was in a very different place from 2008. She had developed a team that was change-ready, which meant that it could swiftly adapt and quickly implement new ways of working to ensure that it could continue delivering the targets, engaging colleagues and responding to customer needs.

Tanya was a good example of applying vital steps to embrace change:

- **Be clear on the reason for change.** Nobody appreciates change for change's sake. Even in a crisis, change fatigue can set in, so make sure that you understand why change is required, and if you're involving others in change, invest heavily in helping them understand why change matters.
- **Adopt a change mindset.** Challenge the status quo. Look for the opportunity in any situation. Be prepared to think differently. Become a possibility thinker to generate a new and better tomorrow.
- **Make change your learning curve.** Be hungry to improve and grow. Develop an insatiable appetite for lifelong learning to increase your capacity for trying something new.
- **Be energized by change.** Recognize the progress you make in the direction of positive change by strengthening your successes and building upon your failings.

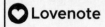 **Lovenote**

Change is the new world order. Develop your change capability to thrive – not just survive – at work.

Safety first

We were invited to deliver a leadership and cultural development programme for an operational division in the retail sector. We met with a range of stakeholders to conduct our customary diagnostic interviews which give us the necessary data upon which any programme is designed. Ahead of the interviews we met with the Senior Director who suggested that in our interviews we put away our laptops and simply engage people in open conversation. The Director indicated that it was a low-trust environment where any external people were viewed with suspicion and formal notetaking might increase the cynicism about our presence.

Sure enough, we were met with a variety of responses, from outright hostility to mild caution. We made it clear that our work would proceed only on the basis that there was sufficient interest and desire to make it work. When we shared our findings with the Director and his HR Director, our primary recommendation was to address the need for creating an environment of psychological safety. We recognized that the only way to deliver meaningful development work was for people to feel safe enough to speak up without the fear of negative consequences. Unfortunately, previous development activity had become associated with delivering organizational efficiencies during which colleagues had lost their jobs. No wonder we were met not with open arms but with mistrust and fear.

In our in-depth interview with Amy Edmondson, Novartis Professor of Leadership and Management at Harvard Business School and author of *The Fearless Organization*, she shared the following:

> To do their best work people need to feel secure and safe in their workplace. I define psychological safety as a shared belief held by members of a team that it is a safe environment for interpersonal risk taking. Individuals feel they can speak up, express their concerns and be heard. This is not to say that people are 'nice'. A psychologically safe workplace is one where people are not full of fear, and not trying to cover their tracks to avoid being embarrassed or punished.

Amy went on to say:

If you don't have psychological safety, it's hard to feel a sense of love for your work. It is comparable to Maslow's Hierarchy of Needs. At the bottom is self-protection which dominates if we are caught up in survival and means that we can't be as focused on and available for our work. When in self-protection our first inclination is to not get hurt, or to get expelled. We tiptoe. We hide our tracks. We try and read the tealeaves. Having psychological safety assumes that your voice is welcome. You go for it, ask your questions, offer your ideas and are available for people.

Amy first developed her research into psychological safety in the hospital sector. There she saw how 'the best teams have a culture where workers feel able to speak up about medical errors, to learn from them and prevent harm to patients' while 'in less effective teams nurses remained silent about the errors they saw'. She concludes: 'In the past two decades hundreds of academic studies about psychological safety have been conducted that measure the positive correlation between psychological safety and desired outcomes such as error reporting, quality improvement and high performance.'

She is the first to admit, however, that a culture of psychological safety is never the easy option: 'Psychological safety feels better than fear, but it's not comfortable. Working in a psychologically safe workplace is a stretch environment. There will be conflict and upset because people will disagree, but it's recognized as necessary to do good work.'

Creating psychological safety has become a starting point for the work we do with leaders, teams and organizations and helping them with their *LoveWork* aspirations. We are not alone. In 2012 Google embarked on an initiative – codenamed Project Aristotle – which set out to answer the following question using data and rigorous analysis: what makes a Google team effective? Over two years researchers conducted in excess of 200 interviews with Googlers (their employees) and looked at more than 250 attributes of over 180 active Google teams. They thought that if they found the perfect mix of traits and skills necessary for a brilliant team, they would solve the problem. What they actually found was: 'Who is on a team matters less than how the team members interact, structure their work and view their contributions' (Google, 2015). They learned that there were five key dynamics which set successful teams apart from other teams at Google, and the number-one factor was psychological safety, defined by Google as 'an individual's perception of the consequences of taking an interpersonal risk or a belief that a team is safe for risk taking in the face of being seen as ignorant, incompetent, negative, or disruptive'.

Where psychological safety doesn't exist, it can create chaos as people run on high anxiety. Some examples of the impact of low psychological safety that we have observed include:

- The leader who was avoided on a Friday afternoon as his quick temper and irritability would spill over onto anyone who crossed his path.
- The leader who was so aggressive in her style that she literally scared people into agreeing with her. She got energy from having a verbal fight, which kept the majority of people around her on tenterhooks.
- The executive committee governed by a manipulative chairperson, which resulted in the team hanging each other out to dry, going behind one another's backs and offering each other platitudes of support which were rarely followed up.

> Psychological safety creates the environment where people can do great work.

Psychological safety starts with an internal decision to have the courage to speak up, have voice, encourage others to take risks, have their back and challenge the status quo.

Ruth was determined to have psychological safety as one of her key success factors for doing the work she loved. As a marketing expert she was used to working in highly competitive environments where people jostled for creative hierarchy and were happy to throw others under the bus to get ahead. She had developed sharp elbows to protect her from the threat of others, but it drained her energy and went against her open and collaborative personality. In our coaching work, Ruth came to the realization that the only way she would fulfil her potential was to step forward and voice what she believed. She started communicating about psychological safety through her social network and introduced it to campaigns at work.

Ruth caught a wave.

With the increased lens on topics such as diversity and inclusion, wellbeing and mental health, psychological safety has gone mainstream. One way of translating it at work is through vulnerability. At work, vulnerability can take many different forms, including:

- speaking up in a meeting to propose a risky or untested idea
- admitting publicly that the project you championed failed, and offering lessons learned in the process
- disagreeing with your boss or offering a different way forward
- willingly giving up time or resources to help out someone on your team, taking away from the resources you have to achieve your own goals
- sticking up for a teammate in the face of unfair criticism
- volunteering to do something you don't know how to do
- showing emotions when you're under pressure or stressed out.

Brené Brown, author of *Daring Greatly* and an expert on social connection, conducted thousands of interviews to discover what lies at the root of social connection (Brown, 2015). A thorough analysis of the data revealed what it was: vulnerability. Vulnerability here does not mean being weak or submissive. On the contrary, it implies the courage to be yourself. It means replacing professional distance and reserve with uncertainty, risk and emotional exposure. Brené describes vulnerability as lying at the root of human connection, which is often missing from workplaces. We suggest that there is a direct correlation between creating environments of psychological safety and vulnerability. Simply put, if you feel safe, you can be vulnerable. If you can be vulnerable, you create deep social connections. By creating social connections, you transcend the notion of work as task so that it becomes an activity imbued with meaning.

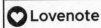

Lovenote

To evolve faster, take risks. To take risks, you need safety.

Learning agility

With a background in law, Julia had a high learning agility for facts and figures. She had developed her cognitive capacity so that she was able to retain large amounts of information at any particular moment. However, she had a low boredom threshold and within a few years of practising law had outgrown the repetition of completing similar transactions. Julia decided to branch out and moved from one of the Magic Circle firms to a media company where she transitioned into the world of marketing. She thrived on the creative element of generating national campaigns, which stretched her to consider things in different ways in order to make something innovative. However, after a few years she was ready for her next challenge and sought out an operational role within the hospitality sector. This meant she needed to develop systems thinking focusing on the interrelationships between things as much as on how things operate. We are not suggesting that you need to demonstrate such high-velocity learning; however, your ability to seek fast learning is essential to the concept behind *LoveWork*.

Someone who shared his passion for learning with us was David Woodward, former CEO Heinz Europe,

How is your work developing you as a person? What is your opportunity to learn? From a personal perspective I have a high learning orientation. However, I chose not to go to university and yet landed up leading very sizeable organisations and presenting in front of Wall Street. At one point in my career one of my terrific bosses challenged me to go to Harvard as a mature student, I was concerned that he was sending me because he had reservations about my performance. When I constructively questioned his motive, he said that the real reason was because he knew I would learn something great and to prepare me for future roles. It was probably the hardest thing I ever did, but it was also one of the most incredible and enriching learning experiences I had. I love to be challenged, but when I attended Professor Michael Porter's classes on strategy it was a whole new level of stretch. For more than three decades, Porter has been developing and refining the essential frameworks that explain how competition works and its implications for strategy in business, government and society. It was a lot to absorb in a few weeks!

Stephen McCall, CEO at edyn, however, challenges our traditional forms of learning and calls out for the need to disrupt the status quo:

Education has a lot to account for when it comes to work. My experience is that the majority of traditional educational methods do not encourage the search for unlocking personal potential. For instance, my daughter has real talent in the creative arts. However, even I worry whether she'll make money from her gift because she's not brilliant at English and maths! Hopefully it won't matter, but it plays on my mind. We need to start at the grass roots to allow students to explore their own potential and to empower them to follow it wherever it takes them. Unfortunately, education systems tend to force people down narrow channels which continues into the job market.

From an organizational perspective Stephen went on to say:

The concept of a company following the same rules and regulations that it always has will not unlock learning. If people are as individualistic and varied as we believe they are then we can't have strict rules which limit them from challenging the status quo. Doing the work you love requires a singular focus about what fulfils you. You will need to be prepared to upset people because not everyone is going to agree with your approach. Companies today need to embrace disruption. I'm proud of the fact that at edyn we are intentionally an open and questioning company. This can cause chaos, but you need to embrace the ups and downs if you go in an open direction. As an organization we allow people to find their own path. We don't want clones. The challenge is, how do we make sure edyn is valued and loved by super creatives as well as analytical introverts?

How do you love to learn? How do you prioritize your learning? How can you accelerate your learning to make you super-relevant in today's disruptive climate? The late educator Sir Ken Robinson was on a mission to transform the culture of education and organizations through a richer conception of human creativity and intelligence. His talk 'Do schools kill creativity?' – the most watched TED Talk of all time – is highly critical of current systems of education, which, he says, are 'based on the manufacturing principles of linearity, conformity and standardization' and 'are failing too many students and teachers alike':

> A primary reason is that human development is not linear and standardized, it is organic and diverse. People, as opposed to products, have hopes and aspirations, feelings and purposes. Education is a personal process. What and how young people are taught has to engage their energies, imaginations and their different ways of learning. (Robinson, 2006)

Ben recounts how, when he left formal education, his goal was to never learn again! Traditional 'learning' did a great job of switching him off education. It wasn't until he stumbled into the field of personal development that his love of learning got ignited. He discovered that he learns by doing. In other words, he needs to have a direct experience of an activity, at which point he can then reflect upon it, take the learning and, if it's relevant, apply it immediately.

Dedicate your work to learning and you will receive
a lifelong reward.

Siân Evans, Director of Leadership and Colleague Experience at Simplyhealth, is a passionate advocate of lifelong learning:

> Be clear about what you have to learn and how you are going to prioritize your learning journey. For instance, be focused about what you are going to learn each year. It's vital to keep up with evolving trends because things change. If you don't keep up and stay relevant, you become yesterday's news. To change yourself and have ongoing impact means that you need to be very intentional about where you spend your time so that you drive forward with what you love to do.

She also shared:

Pay attention to who you are spending your time with. I have changed the influences in my life because when I moved into a new area, I realized I needed to build a new network. I got curious about who was working in my field and developed long-lasting relationships that nourished and supported me.

It's helpful to be aware of the different ways of learning and your own preferences:

- **Visual** – preference for using pictures, images and spatial understanding
- **Auditory** – preference for using sound and music
- **Verbal** – preference for using words, both in speech and writing
- **Kinaesthetic** – preference for using the body and sense of touch
- **Logical** – preference for using logic, reasoning and systems
- **Social** – preference for learning in groups and through relationships
- **Solitary** – preference for learning alone and using self-study.

It's also vital to take ownership for your own learning and find ways to amplify it. In our interview with Wim Dejonghe, Senior Partner at Allen & Overy, he said:

I require intellectual challenge to be fulfilled at work. I am addicted to challenge and look for it all the time. I could have had an easier life for certain but recognize that I need to continue exercising skills on all levels – physical, emotional, relational and intellectual. For instance, I love the challenge of racing a bike against someone, being in a new social environment and building relationships, or having the intellectual stretch of performing in a leadership role where I have to make the judgement calls, push people and get pushed by others.

As well as recognizing your learning preferences, you can apply different techniques to speed up your learning. These have been highlighted in the work of Barbara Oakley, a Professor of Engineering at Oakland University, Michigan, and Terrence Sejnowski, a neuroscientist at the Salk Institute for Biological Studies in San Diego, California. Together they have created what is arguably the world's most successful online course on 'Learning how to learn'. They advocate three different techniques:

1 **Focus/diffuse:** The brain has two primary modes of thinking – a focused mode in which you concentrate on content followed by a diffuse mode, which is a neural resting state in which consolidation occurs, allowing new information to be absorbed by the brain. In the diffuse mode, connections between pieces of information and unexpected insights can occur. That's why people often describe having their best ideas in the shower, on the golf course, jogging, dancing, listening to music – essentially when their brain is in a relaxed place.

2 **Take a break:** To achieve these times of focused- and diffuse-mode thinking, Dr Oakley suggests setting your timer for 25 minutes of focused work, followed by a brief reward which encourages you to go into a relaxed state. We tend to overwork our focused periods by scheduling back-to-back meetings or trying to keep going for too long, which depletes our ability to maximize our learning.

3 **Practice:** 'Chunking' is the process of creating a neural pattern that can be reactivated when needed. It might be a procedure at work, or a narrative for communication. Research shows that having a mental library of well-practised neural chunks is necessary for developing expertise. Chunks build on chunks, and, as Dr Oakley says, the neural network built upon that knowledge grows bigger.

Fast learning is an essential foundation for *LoveWork*. It means that you are constantly seeking ways to improve and become a better version of yourself. It requires you to look at linkages and patterns to improve processes and systems. It demands you to anticipate future trends and to generate different scenarios for responding. Be deliberate about your learning by taking the following steps:

EACH YEAR

Decide on one big learning focus, whether it's related to your personal development like navigating change, or a tangible skill such as using technology in a virtual world.

EVERY MONTH

Set aside an hour to review your personal and work learning and reset your focus.

EACH WEEK

Set aside an hour to review your personal and work learning and reset your focus.

EVERY DAY

Take a moment to note something you have learned to expand your learning mindset

---

 Lovenote

Prioritizing your learning agility rapidly accelerates your ability, capability and sustainability.

Fast and curious

When we ask the majority of people in positions of leadership what is the number-one quality they look for in others there is a consistent response: intense curiosity. The definition of curiosity in the *Oxford English Dictionary* is 'a strong desire to know about something'. Being curious means that, whatever happens, you will be in the best possible place to respond. If there is a crisis, you will go into problem-solving mode to find a way through. If there is an opportunity, you will learn to exploit it. If you are stuck, you will see it as a chance to accelerate your learning. If you are thriving, you will share your learning with others.

Renée Elliott, founder of Planet Organic and co-founder of Beluga Bean, shared:

Learning comes from curiosity. As an adult, learning is about saying, 'I don't know', and being able to admit that you don't know everything. I remember at age 18 I thought I knew everything. Now I realize what I don't know and give myself the permission to explore. Your ability to be open, humble and curious to learn will sustain you in doing the work you love. You can't simply go from university to death without deep learning.

Jonathan Coen, Director of Security at Heathrow, demonstrates high levels of curiosity. His transition from a commercial role to the security space required him to navigate the complexity of knitting together security, intelligence, compliance, training and customer needs. As part of his development into the role, he took part in an intensive psychological profiling exercise which gave him the following feedback:

Jonathan is curious and likes to learn, he will build an awareness of new and different theories and models that are relevant to his area of responsibility and the strategy of the business. He will likely acquire this learning from networking, peer conversations and observations, reading business books, coaching and industry talks, and where relevant will implement and apply approaches that challenge conventional practice … He will bring positive energy to change and his value of 'the art of the possible' drives him to be open and curious to lead movement towards new approaches, models and visions. He has been keen to deliver change to both process and culture across his leadership roles … Jonathan is inquisitive and will ask probing questions to get to the core of an issue. He is open to having his thinking challenged by diverse audiences in order to get as full an understanding as possible.

There is no doubt that a key enabler to Jonathan's success is this ongoing curiosity which he brings to every situation. He describes his purpose as 'the art of the possible', which encourages him to look at everything through a lens of multiple options. This open-mindedness is contagious and means that those in his presence, whether they are senior stakeholders and peers or direct reports and his wider team, all benefit from his infectious curiosity.

A good example was when we started working with his new operational leadership team. Historically, they had been told what to do, with a primary focus on day-to-day tasks. Under Jonathan's leadership he challenged them to think ahead, think differently and think strategically. He scheduled think time in meetings, giving the team space to consider big topics like how they were going to create a great place to work, how they were going to achieve their performance targets and how they were going to operate in sustainable ways. He used provocative terms to get people to lift up. For instance, he talked about thinking at 30,000 feet. Initially, people didn't know what he meant. Where was 30,000 feet? What did it look like? What were the expectations? However, over time they welcomed the approach and started to thrive on the opportunity to apply greater curiosity.

> Being curious helps you navigate any situation.

How do you get curious and stay curious? When you are faced with the unknown, uncertainty and unpredictability, how do you respond? During COVID-19 everyone was faced with unprecedented change. Initially, it was the perfect storm of a global health, socio-economic and business crisis. There were no precedents. There were no clear plans. The longer it went on, the more it impacted business performance and efficiencies as well as personal wellbeing and resilience. Those able to ride the waves of change were fuelled by curiosity. We witnessed people asking new and different questions, creating new ways of working, delivering different services and being energized by the process – despite the level of hardship endured.

Being curious is a foundation for a healthy and rewarding working life. Your ability to translate experiences through a lens of possibility will sustain you through the toughest times and will inspire you to new heights in the good times. However, it is something you need to focus on and develop. Henry Braithwaite, Founder of Lead Forensics, gave his perspective:

> Every day multiple challenges come our way. In my experience, invincible resilience comes from being crystal clear on why you have gone to work that day in the first place. I resonate with the saying: 'There are only two problems in life: 1) you don't know what you want; 2) you know what you want but don't know how to get it.' If you are not able to answer either of these questions, then you are vulnerable to being pushed and pulled by the agendas of other people and getting overwhelmed by conflicting priorities. I have found work harder when I have not been in a learning mode. Staying curious through learning from others, reading books and listening to podcasts helps my mind to be in more positive and resourceful state and keeps me in a discovery mode.

Curiosity engages a portion of the brain's temporal lobe called the hippocampus, says Todd B. Kashdan in a 2009 article called 'Wired to wonder', published in *Greater Good Magazine*. He argues that curiosity has a powerful impact on our cognition, as encountering new ideas and experiences directly transforms our brains, firing neurons and forging new pathways, all the time increasing our capacity for creativity and making new connections. It is, he says, 'the neurological equivalent of personal growth'.

If you're looking for a new role, starting a new one, or falling in love (or back in love) with what you do, curiosity is the ingredient required to make it work. Probably the best way to provoke curiosity is through questions:

If you're looking for a new role you could ask:	If you're starting a new role you could ask:	If you're in the process of falling in love with what you do, or back in love with it, you could ask:
What would a dream role look like?	What does success look like?	What inspires me about my work?
How would I know that I am in the right role?	Who do I need to spend time with?	Why do I do what I do?
What type of company would I love to work with?	What impact do I want to make?	What difference do I want to make?
What kind of people would I enjoy working with?	What do I need to learn?	How would I love others to benefit from what I do?
How could I learn and grow in a new role?	How can I show up with humility and curiosity?	What would make the biggest positive difference to what I do?
What service do I want to provide others?	What quick wins could I deliver?	How could I become even better at what I do?
How could I think differently about a role that would enthuse me?	What is the biggest risk I need to mitigate?	What feedback would I like to hear from others about what I do?

Questions are powerful. Not only does hearing a question affect what our brains do in that instant, it can also shape our future behaviour. Questions trigger a mental reflex known as 'instinctive elaboration'. When a question is posed, it takes over the brain's thought process. And when your brain is thinking about the answer to a question, it can't contemplate anything else. Using questions to stimulate your curiosity opens up possibilities and takes you places you might not have yet contemplated.

 **Lovenote**

Be consistently curious. Ask. Listen. Learn. Thrive.

Adapt

'We want clarity. We want to know what's going on. We want to have crystal-clear priorities. We want to follow the plan. We want one message. We want stability. We want certainty.' Does this sound familiar? If we only heard these messages during the COVID-19 crisis, then it would be understandable. However, these are requests we hear in business on an ongoing basis when in today's volatile, uncertain, complex and ambiguous world it is virtually impossible to provide the level of certainty and detail that people think they need to do their best work. It is essential for organizations to have strategic frameworks to provide clear direction in the form of purpose, values, vision and priorities, but beyond a strong articulation of intent it is nigh impossible to give a step-by-step guide as to what people need to do. This is where the need for adaptability comes in.

In 2019 the management consulting firm Korn Ferry published a report called 'The Self-Disruptive Leader' based on the analysis of 150,000 leadership profiles. They identified five aspects of future-ready leadership, which they called the ADAPT dimensions, encompassing the ability to 'Anticipate, Drive, Accelerate, Partner and Trust'. They noted that 'companies with leaders who aren't future-ready face a double bind: not only are they less able to adapt to the changing business environment, they may face a penalty from those who evaluate their businesses' (Korn Ferry, 2019).

The need to adapt has been especially highlighted in recent decades, with a succession of global crises which have challenged us at every level. In our interview with Richard Boyatzis, the Distinguished University Professor of Organizational Behavior, Psychology, and Cognitive Science at Case Western Reserve University, Cleveland, Ohio, he drew attention to this:

Big events like COVID-19, the wildfires that raged through Australia, or the 7 July 2007 bombings in London give an opportunity to people to ask what is it all about … The evidence suggests that the people who go through these experiences and come out better off have looked at this question. The people who hunker down and just carry on don't get the benefit and suffer more PTSD.

In the face of such massive traumas, many people, he says, simply fall prey to fear and inertia. However, he insists that this can be counteracted:

Our research shows that you need to do things that activate your Positive Emotional Attractor. Individually this includes meditation, yoga, prayer (to a loving god), exercise. There are things you can do with others – laughing, caring for the less fortunate, playing with friends, partners and children. On a spiritual level – reacquainting yourself with a larger sense of purpose. All of those things that you do individually are helped a lot if you are doing or talking about them with other people. The interpersonal reaction around them helps the elevation of hormonal and neurological properties which leads to sustainable benefits. We will see who comes out adapting better and possibly different, or who comes out of COVID-19 feeling battered and damaged with the inevitable waves of PTSD that will happen.

In her interview with us, Amy Edmondson, Novartis Professor of Leadership and Management at Harvard Business School, discussed some of the challenges of adapting:

Dealing with uncertainty is psychologically uncomfortable. For instance, going forward some jobs will be more liable to automation than others. There's no doubt that to love your job you will need to love change. However, change is not something that we naturally love. It is threatening, but it's here to stay. We have to learn to welcome change, live with it and do the best we can. It's very important to not try and do it alone. The future will be a team sport. You will not be alone in working it out. We will be in it together. We will need to talk and figure it out together. We will find things to do. It's not new to our era to see job categories disappear and new ones arise.

Angela Brav, President of Hertz International, also highlighted how our current climate is impacting our reality:

> I am trying to come to terms with what security looks like going forward in a post-COVID-19 world. There is no doubt that the pandemic will change the way we look at work and raises important questions about how to create a sense of safety, belonging and creating bigger and better things in an uncertain world. Will our views about safety change to prioritizing health? Will companies be smaller? Will working from home become a norm and so, will people be as productive? Is it possible to connect through social media as if you are in the office together? We are all being asked to question our fundamental propositions about work.

Adaptation requires a growth mindset.

Learning to adapt starts with an openness and willingness to think and see things differently. It is essential to develop a growth mindset which was made popular through the work of Carol Dweck, the Lewis and Virginia Eaton Professor of Psychology at Stanford University and the author of *Mindset: The New Psychology of Success* (2006). Adopting a growth mindset means that you see challenge as an opportunity to grow, obstacles as things to overcome, and effort as a way to become better at what you do.

We were working with an operational leadership team during the COVID-19 pandemic. They were faced with the very real challenges of maintaining safety, reliability and customer service, while working in a fluid environment with numerous restrictions to hinder their progress. Once they had come through the initial shutdown, which they managed seamlessly as they almost work best in a crisis, they then had to adapt to a 'new norm'. People were forced to work from home and to be apart from team members and colleagues whom they used to spark off every day. Those with children had to juggle home schooling while leading a collective population of several thousand people. They had to absorb constantly changing messaging from the government and filter it through their own political climate.

On a fortnightly basis we conducted a team 'check-in', which consisted of taking a current topic to explore during a video conferencing call. The team leader would set the context by updating the team on the big things on his mind. Typically, this included the latest information from government, organizational priorities and operational requirements. We then asked the team questions such as 'How can you be one step ahead at this time?', 'What would inspire you and your teams during this chapter?' and 'What would help you do your best work right now?' We structured the meeting so that everyone had equal share of voice and then summarized the insight. There were some recurring themes that were essential for people to do their best work:

- Sharing a 'North Star' to provide direction, lift people up and have a common focus.
- Being engaged so as to keep energized, working together and having a sense of belonging.
- Understanding what was most important to accomplish even if it was as short term as a week, or sometimes just by the next day.
- Staying true to the company values such as 'doing the right thing', 'celebrating diversity' and 'keeping everyone safe' so that people felt good about the difference they were making.

As time went on, what became apparent was that the most vital quality for people to develop was adaptability. No one could predict what was going to happen, how long things would take to stabilize, when business would return and what the implications could be. We noticed that team members who in the past had been quite fixed in their attitude were beginning to embrace more flexibility. Requests for specific detail on tasks were being made less frequently. People adjusted to living in the unknown and felt empowered to act based on their own judgement.

A turning point came when the team seemed to self-regulate its own responses to challenges. Rather than 'waiting' for the leader to direct, they were able to anticipate issues, make quick judgements and create opportunities. They managed the flow of knowledge in real time and used agile processes and iterative approaches to rapidly implement ideas. They formed collaborative partnerships based on shared outcomes to exchange ideas, combine complementary capabilities and enable high performance. They welcomed diverse perspectives and used the 'crisis' to accelerate learning and development.

How do you need to adapt to do the work you love? What mindset do you need to adopt? What behaviours do you need to demonstrate? Who can help you along the way? Andreas Thrasy, Chairman of New World Hospitality, shared his recommendations:

> Look for the 'aha' moments. Hang around people who can act like light bulbs and turn on a switch for you. They care. They hold your feet to the fire. It's essential to have a mix of people around you who support and challenge you. I liken it to Edward de Bono's 'Six Thinking Hats' so that you have a team around you covering elements like facts, optimism, caution, possibilities, intuition and thinking.

Andreas went on to give three clear pointers to developing an ability to adapt:

- Challenge your beliefs – because adopting new beliefs opens up windows of opportunity.
- Develop strategies and models to find better ways of working.
- Expand your network to get the right support and challenge.

Part of the reason we – Sophie and Ben – chose to write together was to adapt to changing circumstances. In our increasingly diverse and complex world we felt that bringing together two different perspectives and skillsets would create a better and more meaningful book than if it was just one of us. It encouraged us to test our ideas and put them into action - for instance, with Sophie starting a new job as CEO of The Marketing Society within weeks of starting the book while also navigating COVID-19.

Accelerating your ability to adapt will be one of the most liberating things you can do. It will move you from feeling a 'victim' in work situations to 'owning' your reality, looking at what you can control and influence. It will enable you to move quickly in the face of change so that you make fast decisions and act at pace to ensure you are ahead of the curve. The future will be led by those who can learn and adapt the quickest. Get comfortable with discomfort. Welcome the unknown. Thrive on chaos. Connect with different types of people to seek different perspectives to help you adapt. Seek cognitive diversity to ensure that you think differently and welcome challenge and be prepared to flex your approach every day.

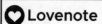 **Lovenote**

The best way to evolve is to adapt.

The future is flexible

Work–life balance. Work–life integration. Work–life fit. Work–life blend. Work–life harmony. Work–life synergy. Flexible working. Home working. Agile working. Depending on the professional or organization using the term, people have been trying to figure out this seemingly illusive problem for years. Until the COVID-19 pandemic, working in a flexible way – including working from home – was often frowned upon by employers. If someone worked from home, they might frequently hear 'supportive' comments such as 'Part-timer!', 'Another half-day?', 'It's all right for some!' or 'Have you got out of your PJs yet?' Also, because the most common day used for home working was Friday, this only increased suspicions about productivity levels.

Even when people came out in support of working from home, they often appeared to be only paying lip service to it, with the underlying message that 'presenteeism' – being seen in the office – was a better way of working. Our perspective was that workers had mixed views on working from home subject to personal situations. Some welcomed the opportunity for the time and space that home working gave them. Others found it isolating and definitely preferred the focus of being in an office and working directly with colleagues.

We believe that a different conversation needs to be had about work and life … what we call 'dynamic working'. When you look at words similar to 'dynamic', including energetic, spirited, active, lively, zestful, vital, vigorous, strong, powerful, positive, effective, enterprising, electric and passionate, and imagine using that as the basis for ways of working, it's a different proposition. The *Oxford English Dictionary* defines 'dynamic' as 'characterized by constant change, activity or progress'. This seems to fit today's world of work which is constantly changing and where the outcome has to be progress.

The impact of 2020's global pandemic has taken the home–work dilemma to a whole new level. In a 2020 *Harvard Business Review* article titled 'Do we really need the office?' Gretchen Gavett writes about how 'COVID-19 has turbocharged this trend [working from home, or WFH]' and that 'both the possibilities and the perils are becoming clearer' (Gavett, 2020). While she admits that 'plenty of research demonstrates that remote work benefits productivity', there are crucial problems we need to face up to, not least of which is that 'this wholesale shift is forcing us to recognize, call out, and reject dangerous norms, such as the "ideal worker" fallacy that disproportionately affects parents and, primarily, women' (Gavett, 2020).

At Accenture, Paul Daugherty, the firm's Chief Technology Officer, thinks that many employees will certainly return to the office eventually – but according to a global survey of its customers, 49 per cent of those who had never before worked from home said they 'plan to do it more often', even after the pandemic eases. He said companies were figuring out how to 'virtualize' every part of work – every meeting, every employee check-in – so that it could potentially be done remotely. 'It has accelerated three years of digital cultural adaptation to three months.'

Leading from the front in the pandemic, Barry Robinson, President and Managing Director, International Operations, at Wyndham Vacation Clubs, shared:

> For those that don't have a home office, making sure you have the right equipment to operate is essential. You need to put time in for yourself and have a routine to break up your day. Although we will be changing our office environment, I expect people to go back to the office for meetings, or to meet in environments where they can get together. Zoom has been fantastic for drop-in meetings, for example – you can make sure more people understand the direction from the top as there are no excuses not to be transparent. We recently conducted a 1,000-person Zoom meeting which I found was very engaging and interactive for all participants.

Nick Dent, Director of Customer Operations at London Underground, shared a personal perspective:

> Prior to COVID I have never worked remotely. I have always needed to provide visible leadership and be with people face to face. I am now open-minded about the benefits that can come from not being dependent on being together in person. For instance, I have teams all over London, working in shifts which historically have been very difficult to access logistically. Now I have weekly calls where I can listen to people directly, share what's on my mind and have the ability to connect regularly. I believe that going forward we won't go back to some of the old ways of working and we need to take the best out of this difficult experience.

Khaled Ismail, Vice President Communications, Europe, Central Asia, Middle East and Africa, at Tetra Pak, insists that we need to 'recognize that the practice of working 9–5 hours is dead' and that 'rethinking the way we work is not a question of if, but when and how'. However, he also raises some crucial issues such as trust and mental health:

> Managers will need to show that they trust people working from home. At the same time they will need to watch out for their teams' mental health and wellbeing as people are working all hours and need support

to create and implement the right boundaries. I expect that these changes will happen by trial and error with different companies and cultures.

Errol Williams, Vice President at WeWork, reinforced the need to redefine the way we work:

> Good economies are employee-centric. COVID-19 has accelerated the shift towards a more permanent period of an employee-centric world of work. As a result, corporations, focus is about how to create the right environment to attract and retain talent. We are seeing massive flexibility being exercised. The idea of where we work has fundamentally changed. For instance, there will be a time when you're at home to think, other times when you can be at an office near your home, and other times when you will need to travel greater distances to be with others and collaborate. What we won't see is a consistent streaming of long commutes every day. I believe a hub-and-spoke model will survive where organizations will have hubs where people can collaborate and spokes where people can work on their own. For this to work, leaders will need to extend trust to employees and focus on output rather than on whether they have clocked in and out.

Indeed, the phenomenon of virtual working raises a host of issues that need to be addressed. For instance, working in a fluid environment presents a blurring of constructs about work, employment, jobs, roles, home, life and relationships. Expectations are changing. The door is wide open about what people want, and challenging the status quo is the norm. Prior to COVID-19 we were running an offsite event for a law firm in a modern London hotel. Following a breakout session the participating lawyers were asked to use the foyer space in the hotel to sit, and this triggered an insightful conversation about the use of their office. In the hotel foyer they were surrounded by the next-generational workforce who were engrossed in their laptops plugged in online. There were countless people seated in every nook and cranny who thrived on being in an open workspace which created a relaxed, social atmosphere for doing business. Contrast this to the law firm which had invested a fortune in leasing plush offices with its own huge foyer that sat empty. It led to a conversation about how to replicate a similar scenario in its own space where people could collaborate alongside each other, generating great ideas and output for clients.

Jonathan Mills, CEO EMEA of Choice Hotels, shared his perspective:

> Coming through COVID has amplified the need to prioritize time for ourselves, our friends and family, and work so that we find the right mix. For instance, one of the challenges I have found is the intensity of working from home being locked in a room morning, evening and night. I believe that the component of balance we need to strive for is having time for ourselves, for the important people in our lives, and making sure that we optimize time for work to make the most of it all.

He went on to say:

> I have found that the challenges I face in work don't go away! In order to address them I believe that you need to be balanced in your approach. You need to keep true to your purpose, manage the volume of work and be clear on expectations. My commitment moving into this new world post-pandemic is balancing how I am going to think differently, be nimble enough to take right action and inspire others. It will also be important to be transparent with the people you work with because you won't have all the answers. It's humbling to convey that and builds trust which is vital to overcoming challenges together.

During the pandemic we were supporting a global company based in the US. The company has a range of functions including operational, commercial, financial, sales and marketing, research and development, and people. As with the majority of companies impacted by lockdown the company shifted to remote working overnight. This offered a range of benefits for some including:

- spending precious time with family members
- saving valuable time in commuting
- having time set aside to progress projects without distractions
- igniting creativity and innovation as a result of needing to think differently.

However, it wasn't straightforward as a range of challenges surfaced:

- increased loneliness, particularly for those who lived on their own
- feelings of disconnection from team members due to the lack of formal and informal contact
- loss of focus and direction with increased task workload and reduced longer-term strategic thinking
- slowing down on personal and career development.

As a consequence we worked together to address these issues in the following ways:

- Scheduling monthly 'check-in' sessions with both the management team and broader leadership team to discuss people issues. We covered areas such as diversity and inclusion, mental health and wellbeing, psychological safety, resilience and collaboration to ensure that everyone had the opportunity to share voice about vital topics which were difficult to progress in the regular daily activity.
- Holding team development sessions to bring individual teams together. We conducted team 'health checks' against various criteria such as prioritization, roles and responsibilities, process and trust. This time strengthened the openness and honesty within teams and, in particular for those who were living on their own, enabled precious connections to be sustained.
- Support for leaders to increase their personal and career development conversations with others. We devised a framework that gave people various touchpoints to reflect upon including leadership, management, coaching, community, safety, fairness, sustainability and technical skills. People devised their own meaningful objectives to accelerate their development, and this not only improved engagement levels but also enhanced succession plans within the company.

The organization in question has a clear strategic plan to double the size of the company over the next few years, to create a great place to work and to be purpose-led in how it engages with colleagues, customers, consumers and community. Implementing this range of interventions during the global COVID-19 pandemic was clear evidence of the executive committee's commitment to doing the right thing, and although the short-term financial implications of the pandemic were tough, it unlocked new levels of thought leadership and engagement which strengthened the company foundations for sustainable growth.

Contrast this with other organizations which were so consumed with survival tactics such as cost cutting, redundancies and restructures that not only did people have to cope with the trauma of losing colleagues and resources, alongside increasing workloads and responsibilities, but there was no time or space to lift up and implement supportive mechanisms such as listening groups, coaching and mentoring to face into the implications of virtual working.

We have identified ten relevant ways to embrace dynamic working.

1 Be proactive

Ensure you are ahead of the curve in naming, defining and exploring dynamic working. Whatever you choose to call our new virtual reality, create the time and space to understand people's current state, what they want and how best to evolve. The rule book has gone out of the window. Working 09:00–17:00 is history. For example, a working parent may choose to be online and available from 09:00 to 13:00, and then again from 15:00 to 18:30, so that the family can spend more quality time outdoors in between home schooling. For someone else (with or without caring responsibilities) a typical 09:00–17:30 workday with only one hour-long break at noon may work better. Alternatively, continuing your 'day' in the evening once the kids are asleep can complement an earlier end time (such as a 07:00–15:30 schedule which picks up again around 19:00).

2 Be outcome-oriented

Recognize that achieving agreed goals is the name of the game, rather than the process of what it looks like to get there. It's critical to get on the same page about what success looks like using the language that has meaning for others (e.g. priorities, metrics, targets, goals) – in other words, what's important and what matters most. Involving people in defining the outcomes to deliver ensures ownership and adds another level of meaning to the process. It's also essential to recognize and celebrate success along the way. One of our favourite mantras is 'progress not perfection', which keeps people energized along the path of success, rather than waiting for the final outcome.

3 Be trusting

In March 2019 the website *Great Place to Work* published data from more than 100 million employees and over 30 years of research that shows, 'Trust is what ultimately makes a truly great employer – regardless of size, industry, or region of the globe. Trust means giving people the autonomy to get on and deliver.' The Great Place to Work Trust Model consists of five dimensions:

1 **Credibility** – where people see management as believable and trustworthy
2 **Respect** – where people feel involved in decision making
3 **Fairness** – where people believe management practices and policies are fair
4 **Pride** – where people feel proud about the impact of their individual work, as well as the company
5 **Camaraderie** – where people believe the company has a strong sense of community and is a welcoming place to be.

From our perspective trusting also means: stopping micromanaging, as this undermines people's confidence and capability; having open and honest conversations about performance; giving real-time feedback focused on playing to strengths; and doing things differently to deliver better outcomes.

4 Be transparent

Build a culture of psychological safety where everyone feels able to speak up about what's working/not working and can offer possible solutions. Best ideas can come from anyone and anywhere. Break down hierarchy so that everyone has a sense of belonging and that their opinion matters – because it does. Make sure that information flows freely between people and teams. In this age of uncertainty, communication is the glue that makes things stick. Even if you don't have all the answers (and you won't), it's essential to communicate what you can and can't in a straightforward approach.

5 Be vulnerable

Vulnerability is the new strength at work. As Amy Edmondson, Novartis Professor of Leadership and Management at Harvard Business School, writes in *The Fearless Organization*: 'I would like to suggest a few simple, uncommon, powerful phrases that anyone can utter to make the workplace feel just a tiny bit more psychologically safe: I don't know. I need help. I made a mistake. I'm sorry. Each of these is an expression of vulnerability' (Edmondson, 2018).

6 Be inclusive

Everyone is different. Everyone has individual needs and wants, which means that it is vital to understand others' preferences and adapt accordingly. This starts with yourself. What do you need and want to thrive in a virtual economy? It's useful here to recall Abraham Maslow's well-known Hierarchy of Needs. This starts by considering your and others' physiological needs like ergonomics so that people's workspaces are designed for maximum interactivity along with the right technology to enable performance. Next up are safety needs such as personal security, employment, health and wellbeing. There is heightened sensitivity about security and employment, as the COVID-19 crisis throws millions of people across the globe out of work. Nurturing health and wellbeing demands an extra focus in a virtual environment, as it is challenging to meet physical, emotional, mental and spiritual requirements. The next need is love and belonging. This includes friendship and having a sense of connection, which we see as one of the biggest areas negatively impacted by working virtually. Love and belonging are fundamental to our ability to thrive and be creative, so watching out for isolation and loneliness is important. One step up the hierarchy is the need for esteem and gaining the necessary appreciation and recognition from others to boost our personal belief. Finally, at the top of Maslow's Hierarchy of Needs is self-actualization – the need to fulfil our potential and to become all that we can be. Although some people are thriving in the virtual environment, we believe that there will need to be a healthy mix of together and remote working to create the optimum conditions for inclusion.

7 *Be connected*

The COVID-19 pandemic has made the absence of socialization stark for most workers. From team meetings and one-to-ones to casual conversations, serendipitous encounters or drinks after work, the opportunity to connect has real value beyond the ability to innovate and solve problems. It supports our need for engagement and connection at work. Research from Missouri University of Science and Technology shows that 'remote teams benefit from physical interaction by coming together at least once a year to solidify social bonds that then improve teamwork'. Whether you are leading or working with others it helps to learn about their communication preferences. How do they like to keep in touch? Text? Email? Chat? Scheduled video calls? Ad-hoc contact? Even a telephone call! It's vital to use a range of channels to strengthen connection. Joel Burrows, CEO at Ghirardelli, is highly attuned to the need for connection. He shared: 'Following the global pandemic there will be more scope for flexible working. Technology will continue to improve, enabling a seamless experience connecting online. It will require more planning to have great meetings online as we learn how to use technology to make it happen.'

8 Be compassionate

In a fast-moving dynamic environment one of the attributes most valued by people is to show you care. This is best demonstrated through compassion, which is anticipating others' situations and showing that you understand. It is applying acceptance and forgiveness when people make mistakes. It's about assuming good intent before jumping to conclusions. Jeff Weiner, the Executive Chairman at LinkedIn, describes compassion as 'empathy plus action'. In a 2018 Wharton Undergraduate Commencement entitled 'Be compassionate', he said: 'I would aspire to manage compassionately. That meant pausing, and being a spectator to my own thoughts, especially when getting emotional. It meant walking a mile in the other person's shoes; and understanding their hopes, their fears, their strengths and their weaknesses. And it meant doing everything within my power to set them up to be successful.'

9 Be authentic

In dynamic working there is no space for pretence. Everything is moving too fast. Information is flowing freely. Data rules. Technology – artificial intelligence, automation, digitalization and robotics – continues to accelerate. Yes, we need to adapt, but it needs to be grounded in our authentic selves. Being authentic means having a high level of self-awareness – as Socrates said, 'To know thyself is the beginning of wisdom.' Authenticity engenders trust as people know what they are getting.

10 Be intentional

In a 2020 *McKinsey Quarterly* article titled 'The CEO moment: Leadership for a new era', we were intrigued to see Michael Fisher, President and CEO of Cincinnati Children's Hospital Medical Center, sharing how he has begun to be explicit about what is on his 'to do' and 'to be' lists. As Fisher explains:

I never purposefully gave thought to whether there's a way to be really intentional about how I want to show up every day. So I've added a 'to be' list to my repertoire. Today, for example, I want to be generous and genuine. I hope I'm that way every day. But today, I want to make sure it stays top of mind. On a different day this week … I knew that part of my job was to be collaborative and catalytic. So I pick out two qualities, two kinds of 'to be', every morning as part of my normal routine. (Fisher, 2020)

We have been advocates of being intentional and making 'to be' lists for many years. It is vital to be clear about your intention because intention inspires outcome. In other words, deciding how you want 'to be' is the first step to making it a reality.

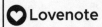 **Lovenote**

As the late great Ella Fitzgerald sang: 'T'aint what you do, it's the way that you do it, and that's what gets results.'

At the heart of it

Evolution is popularly construed as the 'survival of the fittest'.

Surviving a rapidly changing world is one thing; thriving in
that world is another, and our higher goal.

Accepting the importance of evolution in business and
people is essential. Learn to love change and you will love
work more.

Change feels dangerous for many,
so a 'safety-first' approach is needed.

Make psychological safety a priority.

The future of work will require dynamic ways of thinking and
dynamic ways of working to
navigate the inevitability of change.

To evolve, we must adapt.
To adapt smartly and at pace requires
'agility ability' – nimble thinking at the forefront of change.

We must be constantly curious about the benefits of
change, iteration and improvement,
and not just accept but accelerate evolution.

STAGE 3

Deliver

Let's check in with our journey so far. In Stage 1: Discover, we focused on the analysis and insight to create the foundation of self-knowledge:

- Our **first step** (Chapter 1) looked at 'why' (defining your purpose).
- Our **second step** (Chapter 2) articulated your 'what' (your inspiring vision and the direction you want to go).
- The **third step** (Chapter 3) uncovered your code – your 'how'.

We then moved on to Stage 2: Develop, encouraging you to test and challenge your thinking to expand your impact and influence:

- Our **fourth step** (Chapter 4) supported you to unlock your potential for doing the work you love.
- Our **fifth step** (Chapter 5) reminded you that relationships are at the heart of work and the quality of them determines the quality of your work.
- Our **sixth step** (Chapter 6) challenged you to adapt at pace as it is essential in ongoing times of change.

We now move on to the final part, Stage 3: Deliver, which will enable you to apply and iterate your approach to make work consistently better.

7
Make it matter

The impact question

Ben had a love–hate relationship growing up at the Yehudi Menuhin School. Being at the most famous music school in the world was considered a privilege for many and yet he wanted out. Playing the violin all day did not fulfil his deepest desires or help him to make sense of the world. Enter Sally Trench. One of the best things the school offered was introducing students to a wide range of people and their life experiences. Sally came to share her extraordinary story at the school. During her chain-smoking talk, Ben was gripped.

Born in suburban Surrey at the end of World War II, Sally grew up in London in a conventional, successful middle-class family. Her father – Sir Peter Edward Trench – was in the housing industry and at one point was the Managing Director of Bovis. The family would spend the week in St John's Wood, north London, and weekends at a country house near Billingshurst, Sussex. Yet Sally's early life was so troubled – both parents worked, and she was brought up by a nanny – that she says she has now almost entirely blocked out memories of her first ten years. 'I am sure I was to blame,' she records in her memoir (Trench, 1968), 'but I felt trapped, unhappy and terribly unloved. I suffered ghastly emotional pain, and the more unhappy I became, the more badly I behaved.' On her seventh birthday, for instance, she was given a watch, which she promptly stamped into the floor. At 15, when her elder brother was made head boy of Ampleforth College, she was expelled from her fifth convent school. She said: 'I was the obvious humiliation of parental expectation. The more I rebelled, the worse my relationship with my parents became' (Trench, 1968).

Yet despite, or because of, this unhappiness, she grew up with what she describes as 'a sense of mission'. After her fifth and final expulsion from school, she began to look for a cause. She found it at Waterloo station in London. Late one night in the early 1960s, making her way home after a party, Trench noticed a group of homeless men and women settling down to sleep on newspapers. 'I was looking rather smart,' she recalls, 'and I thought, God, how disgusting! But then I had a thought: Hang on, I'm meant to be a Christian. I must do something. So I went and sat down …, offered cigarettes and began to make conversation' (Trench, 1968). Among the homeless at Waterloo she found not only a cause but kinship. She began to visit them secretly at night, bicycling six miles from her parents' home with coffee and blankets. Then she took to the streets, living either in squats and derelict buildings with addicts or on bomb sites with meths drinkers, many of them war veterans debilitated by combat trauma.

This rootless, precarious existence could not be sustained for ever. After four years, Trench found herself in a mental hospital, recovering from exhaustion. As a therapy, she started work on a memoir of her time on the streets. *Bury Me in My Boots* became one of the bestsellers of 1968, eventually selling more than a million copies. 'From walking the streets of London being called a whore because of what I looked like and who I lived with,' she says, 'I became Joan of Arc of bloody England. Here was an intelligent, bright-eyed, not unpretty girl from an upper-class background who had gone to live with the homeless. It was a media paradise of a story, and did they make something of it.'

By the time Sally came to speak at the Yehudi Menuhin School she had used her royalties from the book to set up Project Spark in the early 1970s. Originally, Spark offered a safety net to young people who were in danger of sinking into a life of drug addiction and crime. Spark offered a mixture of practical help and 'tough love' to restore self-respect and offer children a realistic and rewarding future. Ben would go and spend time at Sally's home in West London where Spark was housed, mixing with the young people who benefited from her care and compassion. The environment was a massive contrast to the privileged world of classical music, but it was there that he first discovered his passion for helping others.

Life is too short to do work that doesn't make a positive difference and fulfil your personal mission. In these unprecedented times it becomes an even bigger imperative for everyone to take responsibility to make a tangible difference to help people, support the planet and create profit in the process. In our interview with Richard Boyatzis, Distinguished University Professor at Case Western Reserve University, he articulated the importance of creating the foundations for making a meaningful impact:

> It doesn't matter where you are on the socio-economic spectrum, you have the opportunity to set a vision and make progress versus wasting a life. Dreaming is important, but it is hard if you have been beaten, oppressed, or you are a member of a visible minority. However, it doesn't mean it's not possible. Although the drive has to come from within you, don't do anything alone. Make psychological contracts with your own personal board – create a collection of people including mentors, coaches, friends and family to support you in the realization of your vision.

Someone who has invested large amounts of personal and professional time exploring impact is Emily Chang, CEO, China, at McCann Worldgroup. She shared:

> Legacy is such a big word. It can bring to mind sombre financial decisions made in quiet moments of solitude. Or, on the other hand, larger-than-life characters who have achieved such heights of which most of us can never dream. But it's worth remembering that each of us was made to leave a legacy. We weren't created to float through this life, leaving things untouched. Rather, we are here to do exactly the opposite. Not just to touch, but to play, experiment, support, shape, craft and cradle. We are here to make an impact, to leave things better than we found them.

Laura Miller, Executive Vice President, Chief Information Officer, at Macy's, gave her perspective:

Whether it's making a difference to a company, team or individual there are some days that you feel caught up on the hamster wheel and you are spinning so hard that it's hard to recognize the impact you can make. When this happens, I have to remember that what makes the difference for me is to enhance the lives of others. If I can help one person's work become easier or make them more successful, I have fulfilled my purpose that day.

Another valuable insight came from Wim Dejonghe, Senior Partner at Allen & Overy:

Probably the best advice I've received about life, which can be applied to work as well, is the idea that you are the architect of your own life and therefore you must take control. Obviously, it's easier when [you are] in a privileged position to do this. However, anyone in a business environment can be the architect of their lives and career path. I don't believe in making big career plans − I didn't plan to be where I am but by being open-minded and willing to change, my work evolved. I have learned that if something doesn't make you happy, move on. It's vital to be happy with what you do as work is such a big part of life. You can create your own opportunities. Don't just be passive or reactive − take the initiative and be bold. In my career, it has always been a positive decision to stay or to move on with my career rather than just be in cruise mode.

Wanting to have an impact and make a difference are fundamental human drivers. The critical questions to ask are: What impact do you want to have? What difference do you want to make?

Samira was a successful engineer in the technology sector. She was driven to deliver big objectives for her company and quickly moved up through the ranks to a senior executive role. Married to a loving wife, Samira enjoyed all the trappings of an executive lifestyle − global travel, luxury hotels and a generous expense account. When we met Samira, we might have expected to hear a happy story. However, instead it was an all too familiar account of high stress, relentless demands and physical exhaustion underpinned by a sense of longing for something more meaningful. The more Samira accumulated in terms of worldly goods, the more she questioned what she was doing and where she was going.

We asked Samira what drove her and what difference she wanted to make. She didn't know. Samira came to the realization that she had never stopped long enough to ask these important questions and as a consequence had focused on external influences to guide her work and life. It was now time to turn her attention inward and discover what impact she wanted to have.

We encouraged Samira to reflect upon a series of potentially life-changing questions. These are closely linked to those associated with the discovery of purpose we looked at in Chapter 1 but are specifically reformulated here for the world of work:

What impact do you want to have through your work?

What difference do you want to make as a result of your work?

What value do you want to add from your work?

What legacy do you want to leave as a consequence of your work?

Samira took these questions to heart. She described her purpose as 'making a difference', but exploring these areas challenged her to quantify what she meant. As Samira dug deeper into her intrinsic motivations, she realized that although she loved achieving results and getting stuff done, there was a gap in terms of *why* she was doing it. Through her exploration, what began to emerge was a desire to help others do better work and have better lives. We challenged Samira to continue defining what this would mean and look like. She referenced one of her team members as a good example. Nina was a single mother who had weathered tough times through a divorce and the need to prove herself in a male-dominated tech industry. Samira spotted Nina's potential to grow and excel and made it part of her mission to ensure Nina could overcome any of the roadblocks that would come her way.

There was a culture of presenteeism in the organization which Samira knew would be a hurdle for Nina as she tried to progress. Although Samira took a strong stand against the need to 'be seen' at work versus being measured on results, there was a legacy culture that meant if you left work on time, it would be accompanied by comments like 'Part-timer!', 'Another half-day!', 'Thanks for showing up!'. Samira had tried to remove these behaviours through constant messaging about the need to work in dynamic ways as well as role-modelling flexible ways of working, but when she asked Nina about her future ambition and what it would take to get her there, Nina made it obvious that she didn't think her dreams could be achieved in such a judgemental environment.

Fuelled by her commitment to helping others do better work and have better lives, Samira decided to tackle presenteeism head on. She engaged with her line manager who was renowned for having an insatiable work appetite. It was not an easy topic to broach, but, again driven by her desire to make a difference, Samira persevered with her boss and enquired about the type of legacy he wanted to leave and how she could help him achieve it. This line of questioning disarmed her manager, who admitted that it was rare for anyone to take the time to understand him in more depth. He talked about his own heroes, who had created not only innovative technology but also great places to work. This opened up a conversation about how they could emulate some of these accomplishments in their current environment. Samira shared the experience of someone like Nina who was being unintentionally thwarted in her quest for success, and her boss became committed to breaking down barriers so that everyone could fulfil their potential.

Together, Samira and her boss set up listening groups to get under the skin of what was going on. It soon became apparent that although people thrived on the level of ambition within the company, there were fears about not keeping up and the implications of this for career progression. Samira collated the data, formed a steering group and set in motion a series of initiatives to change the culture, which included:

- training and development to raise awareness and upskilling in dynamic ways of working
- implementing different communication channels to ensure transparency of progress and challenges
- new ways of managing performance so that numerical ratings were disbanded, making way for great conversations which focused on individual preferences rather than generic indicators which failed to take into account the diversity within the organization.

Samira's work world changed. She started to feel that she was genuinely helping people do better work and live better lives as a consequence of her actions. This spilled out into own life where she was able to replicate this aspiration in her own community. Having been a passive citizen, Samira now enjoyed focusing on a big issue each year, including racism, wellbeing and education, which gave her life another dimension.

Choose the impact you want to have.

One of the most impactful stories we've ever read is that of Edith Eger who survived the Holocaust to go on to be a renowned psychologist and specialist in the treatment of post-traumatic stress disorder. In 1944, aged 16, Edith was sent to Auschwitz concentration camp. Separated from her parents on arrival, she endured unimaginable experiences, including being made to dance for the infamous Josef Mengele, also known as the Angel of Death. When the camp was finally liberated, Edith was pulled from a pile of bodies, barely alive. Edith wrote her unforgettable story in *The Choice*. In her words:

> Though I could have remained a permanent victim ... I made the choice to heal. Early on, I realized that true freedom can only be found by forgiving, letting go, and moving on... I will forever strive to help people make the choice to heal and thrive. That's a promise!! (Eger, 2017)

Edith's words are echoed in our interview with Richard Boyatzis, Distinguished University Professor at Case Western Reserve University, who referenced examples of his executive doctoral students who have turned their vision into action:

> If you have created your larger vision, then one of the things to think about are the moves that you could be making now that would make your vision possible. For instance, my executive doctoral students' average age is 49. They all have big jobs and families. What they often say is that they would like to do some teaching at university once they have their doctorate. One of the things that blows them away is that they are already adding 20–30 hours a week by attending their doctoral programme. Therefore I encourage them to start networking with the colleges that are within a one-hour drive to where they live to explore teaching a course. I tell them to see what it's like, develop a network and remind them that if they do well, people will love it. They wouldn't have thought about taking these steps and gaining experience about being a professor until they had finished their course, rather than during it. This helps them move closer to their vision and the difference they want to make.

A perspective of patience comes from Bill Gates; we support his point of view that 'most people overestimate what they can accomplish in a year – and underestimate what they can achieve in a decade.' In other words, allow your impact to evolve over time so that your work becomes an expression of your deepest desires.

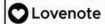 **Lovenote**

What impact do you want to have? It's a choice only you can make.

Switching on the stretch zone

One of the main themes from our interviews with people who had discovered the work they love was the importance of challenging yourself to learn and grow. Renée Elliott, founder of Planet Organic and co-founder of Beluga Bean, expressed it in the following way:

> Today I am out of Planet Organic and my new business is about self-knowledge. It's about helping people discover what they are passionate about, what they are really good at and what they can express in the world. The question I challenge people with is: 'Where can you be on purpose and make a difference?' I am still driven by making things better. I want to do better work, have a better life and make a meaningful contribution while I'm earning.

She insisted that: 'Loving your work is about living your truth, following your passion, getting behind things that you really believe in and influencing others to get behind them. Work is not about a goal or destination.' For her, growth has never been about chasing a goal: 'It was about the journey and staying in the moment along the way as it is the only thing that matters. It is in the present where clarity and fulfilment lie.'

Amy Edmondson, Novartis Professor of Leadership and Management at Harvard Business School, spoke strongly about the importance of challenge: 'In order to do what you love it is vital to stretch, experiment and try new things.' She outlined three approaches to challenging yourself and accelerating your learning:

1 Find development opportunities in doing work that matters.
2 Stretch yourself to the point where it's almost a strain – make sure your work is a stretch and that you are doing things you haven't done before.
3 Set things up so that you are working with people who are different from you in background, personality, expertise and approach.

Andreas Thrasy, Chairman at New World Hospitality, told us he felt a kind of desperation to change and grow:

> Desperation led me to rethink my approach and took me outside my frame of reference. There was something burning inside me that opened up my mind, tapped into my creativity and I got inspired. As a result, I created the brand 'My Hotels'. It's the challenges in life that spur me on. I

have found that, once in flow, it's essential to continue breaking down old beliefs and habits in order to learn better ways.

Mike is a great example of someone who challenges himself to stretch, experiment and try new things. With a relatively conventional background – his parents were teachers – Mike grew up in a quiet suburb. He left school with few formal qualifications, and rather than apply himself to university, together with a friend he had the dream of becoming an entrepreneur and developing his own business. His friend had a small amount of family money that he used as seed funding, and they came up with an idea to generate sales online. As Mike is the first to admit, they made virtually every mistake in the book in starting a new business, but what kept them going was a fundamental belief in the goodness of their service, which created massive value for both customers and colleagues.

Mike and his friend stretched themselves to breaking point in achieving their initial goals and paid a price in terms of their health and marital relationships. However, on completing on the sale of their first business and making several million each in the process, they were able to reset and leverage their experience. When we started working with Mike, he was clear about where he had been but wanted to challenge himself even more to continue his accelerated path in a sustainable way. This involved several factors, including the creation of a longer-term vision, evolving a roadmap for his family, work and life, and doing the groundwork for the educational foundation he wanted to form. Mike dug deep into his own sense of purpose and found it informative and energizing to apply his big why to his decision making. In terms of his family, he deliberately set aside time to be with his children and found it deeply meaningful to be actively engaged in their lives.

In the evolution of their next business Mike and his partner prioritized bringing together a diverse team who could bring the necessary discipline and structure to their ideas to scale the organization in bigger and better ways. He set aside some start-up money for his educational foundation and broadened his network with like-minded people who shared his passion for providing early opportunities for the next generation to learn in experiential ways.

Mike thrived on challenge and found that he was constantly refreshed by whatever came his way rather than feeling the permanent frustration that he used to experience. When we asked him what made the difference, he said that it was a combination of factors, including the synthesis of his purpose, vision, values, strengths and relationships, mixed with large doses of curiosity that propelled him forward.

From a work perspective David Woodward, former CEO Heinz Europe, shared valuable insight into how he constantly challenges and stretches himself and the organizations he works for: 'I believe in taking calculated risk, which has helped me to go beyond what I thought was possible.' In the context of Heinz, he gave a wide number of examples, ranging across product innovations, organizational structures such as 'a department known as Core and Explore ... dedicated to innovation freed from P&L responsibilities', and the fast-track promotion of 'latent and atypical talent'. He concluded:

Not taking an overly cautious approach has benefited me and the companies I have worked with as long as I diligently run decisions through three lenses: 1. Economic – Will the decision make money? Is it a sensible move? 2. Legal – is it fully legal in the country / sector we are operating in ? Are we doing the right thing? 3. Social – What's the impact on the society and community around us? Will it support others in a sustainable way? I have found that too many people focus on the money and then move on. It's vital to focus on all three component parts.

What are the reference points you use to thrive on challenge? In our conversation with Staynton Brown, Director Diversity and Inclusion and Talent at Transport for London, he said:

I believe it's important to take calculated and controlled risks when developing your work. People often talk to me about the desire to progress. I ask them, 'Why do you want to progress?' This helps them get behind the status stuff and to start seeing their work as an extension of their life. I believe it's important to be willing to take sideway moves, change organizations and embrace your work in multidimensional ways.

Staynton referenced the poignant insight given by the palliative care nurse Bronnie Ware in her book *The Top Five Regrets of the Dying*. In this book Bronnie shares conversations she had with dying patients about any regrets they had or anything they would do differently. One of the most common regrets was expressed as 'I wish that I had let myself be happier'. As Bronnie wrote, 'Many did not realise until the end that happiness is a choice. They stayed stuck in old patterns and habits' (Ware, 2012). She went on to say: 'Life is a choice. It is YOUR life. Choose consciously, choose wisely, choose honestly. Choose happiness.'

In his mentoring, Staynton said that he challenges people to recognize that they have more choices than they care to admit and to make sure that they don't look back on their life with regret.

Personal challenge comes in many different shapes and sizes, and expanding your realm of challenge does not mean that you need to find new work. COVID-19 has taken the level of challenge people are experiencing at work to new heights. One industry hit more than most during the pandemic was aviation, with passenger numbers dropping more than 80 per cent. In our interview with John Holland Kaye, CEO at Heathrow, he described how he and his team responded to the fast-changing circumstances 'navigating without a map ... working with our values and instinct':

> It forced us to pick up as many clues and insight as we could. We needed to be open to amending the plan when things changed. We regrouped by starting with the end in mind and created forecasts to guide us going forward. In our case we focused on passenger numbers and built an organization about what it might look like in 12–18 months. I believe that you need to plan ahead. Once you have a plan, you need to stick to it until you have a new plan. In other words the plan is the plan until there is a new plan.

Responding to challenge and stretching in this way was far from comfortable, he admits:

> COVID-19 triggered an extremely challenging dilemma between protecting jobs or legacy pay. It compared to the financial crisis when I was with a different company and we were facing extreme difficulty

with costs. I was the commercial director at the time and had to write to suppliers asking them to take a cut. This act put considerable pressure on our supply chain, some of whom were small companies and who suffered as a consequence. The decision acted as a blunt instrument which did not sit comfortably with me. Therefore when we went into planning to navigate coronavirus, I decided to protect people's jobs to help take away the barriers for their progress. On this occasion we committed to pay our suppliers within 30 days and asked them to do the same as it was the right thing to do. It was important to not just champion our supply chain in the good times but also when times are tough.

Although most challenge is uncomfortable, as it stretches you to think and behave differently, the healthy part of challenge is that it helps you develop new capability and broaden your horizons. For instance, each book we write challenges us to the very core in terms of our knowledge, experience and ability to communicate ideas in clear and compelling ways.

How much challenge do you need to love the work you do? Find out your challenge quotient. Calibrate when too much challenge can become a block to doing the work you love as the stress becomes too great. Recognize, too, when there is insufficient challenge, as this will demotivate and drain you, and drive your own level of challenge to thrive at work.

❤**Lovenote**

Finding your 'sweet spot of stretch' every day helps you work, rest and play.

Deep and meaningful

One of the most fundamental requirements to do the work you love is its deeper meaning. In their 2013 article 'Increasing the "meaning quotient" of work' for the *McKinsey Quarterly*, Susie

Cranston and Scott Keller's research shows that the ingredient people believe is missing for them at work is having a strong sense of meaning, a sense that what they do is original, really matters, and will make a difference to others. What if you were to see work as an opportunity to create meaning and as a result were in a position to make a genuine difference? Angela Brav, President, Hertz International, discovered meaning through developing others:

> I have drawn meaning from learning that your real value as a leader is to create an environment which enables others to flourish. When your team isn't distracted with 'surviving' they can be freed up to find 'new and better ways' to deliver results. Great leaders focus on creating a vision and the conditions that enable others to generate solutions.

Laura Miller, Executive Vice President, Chief Information Officer, at Macy's, shared a similar perspective about deriving meaning from supporting others:

> Leadership is a role to take seriously and means that you need to be committed to serving others. As a leader it's important that you love helping others. If not, you are just fulfilling your ego. Leadership requires you to let others have the credit and lift them up. It is not all about you.

Jonathan Coen, Director of Security at Heathrow, was also clear about the significance of meaning:

> Life is a combination of emotional memories. Therefore I want to create meaningful memories. For instance, if I am creating great experiences for passengers and colleagues, I am enhancing their lives. However, if I am just transacting and stamping out process, then not surprisingly I find it harder to emotionally connect. I have come to recognize that I need to make work a series of emotional connections and that the act of creating memorable experiences for colleagues and customers does just that.

Several years ago we ran a leadership development programme at Heinz championed by David Woodward, former CEO Heinz Europe. Entitled 'Game-changing Leadership', the programme engaged over 1,000 colleagues, ranging from those working on the frontline in the factory through to those sitting on the Executive Committee. David was very clear about the strategic intent behind the programme, at the heart of which was the recognition that 'everyone is a leader'. He talked passionately about leadership not being a role, title, position, grade or paycheck but a mindset characterized by taking initiative and challenging the status quo. David and his leadership team felt very strongly about creating meaning at work. He sensed that although people had tremendous affinity with the Heinz brand and love of its iconic products such as Heinz Tomato Ketchup and Heinz Baked Beanz, there was an opportunity to unlock another level of passion.

We believe strongly that, whatever your circumstances at work, it's vital to recognize that it is within your control to give it the meaning you choose. Stuart was in a high-pressured sales role, accountable for the majority of customer acquisitions in a company that was focused on achieving a number which no one thought was possible. When we started coaching Stuart he was on the verge of burnout. Working excessive hours and feeling constantly stressed, he was consumed with a fear of failure that dominated his state of mind.

To explore the meaning Stuart was giving to the situation and the resulting impact it was having, we used a simple cognitive tool based on the ABC model created by Albert Ellis, an American psychologist who in 1955 developed rational emotive behaviour therapy (REBT):

- 'A' stands for **Activating Event**.
- 'B' represents **Belief**.
- 'C' is for **Consequences**.

Stuart was clear that the Activating Event was the expectation that he would deliver the sales target, even though it had never been done before. His Belief was that he was reliant on others, as it was a team effort, yet he didn't feel that he had sufficient alignment to make it happen. The Consequence was high anxiety as he felt alone and at risk of not delivering. We challenged Stuart on his interpretation of the situation and the meaning he was giving it. What if he gave it a different meaning which led to a different consequence?

In situations like this it's helpful to apply 'possibility thinking'. The premise is that you generate various options for consideration and, in doing so, open your mind to different alternatives. Stuart explored several possibilities, including how to strengthen collaboration with colleagues through being open and vulnerable to generate understanding; how to generate a compelling vision and narrative to excite people and create engagement over and above delivering the target number; and how to reset expectations with his line manager. The simple act of exploring options helped Stuart to give the target a different meaning and see that he could do something about it.

Stuart asked us to conduct a 360-degree feedback process where we went to his key stakeholders and got honest views about how he was coming across and what they would advise him to do differently. The messages were clear. Everyone valued Stuart's energy, drive and tenacity but found him too stubborn, aggressive and narrow-minded. This mirrored his personal reflection and gave him the platform to reset his relationships with colleagues. By taking these steps Stuart was able to form a different meaning for his work, moving from 'threat, fear and impossible' to 'opportunity, challenge and growth'. Thankfully, Stuart and his team did go on to achieve and then surpass their sales target, but, more importantly, the process created a new sense of belief in the company about what was possible and how to achieve it.

On a larger scale we have witnessed multiple cases of where people and organizations have had to search for meaning to help navigate the COVID-19 pandemic. A range of our clients – working in industries such as aviation, transportation, hospitality and retail – were in the direct firing line. They had to jump into crisis management and weather the storm of managing their operating costs while contending with a drastic drop in customer numbers. They needed to help employees deal with unprecedented levels of insecurity about the future, as well as equipping them to work from home and perform in the present. At the right time we worked with them to engage people in conversations about topics such as purpose, vision, strengths, resilience, wellbeing, leadership and inclusion to provide a broader context and to understand how they could make the best of the situation. In fact, the need to accelerate learning and development became a priority as people needed to adopt different mindsets and acquire new skills so that they were fit for the future.

Cheryl is a powerful example of how to frame a crisis in a way that provides the strength, energy and grit to face it with humility, vulnerability and adaptability. Heading up a factory operation that was able to continue during the COVID-19 pandemic, Cheryl had to swiftly implement vital safety precautions, keep production going, and help employees decide on the right course of action to safeguard their health and roles, alongside advising the organization on output levels. On top of it all, Cheryl's appointment had already been questioned by some long-term employees who were challenged by having a woman in an operational leadership role. During the pandemic the 'Movement for Freedom, Liberation and Justice' triggered by the death of George Floyd meant that Cheryl had the opportunity to address racism and educate people about diversity and inclusion inside her organization.

While supporting Cheryl, we encouraged her to step back from the daily firefighting and clarify her vision of what she wanted the crisis to mean. In her soul, she knew that it gave her the platform to implement changes that were long overdue, which for various reasons had been out of bounds. Now she could quickly move to modernize working practices, increase operational resilience and ensure equal employment opportunities. She needed to get her leadership team on board because there was a history of low trust and lack of understanding.

We conducted some initial virtual sessions where we facilitated open conversations about what was going on, the direction the team wanted to go and how they could work together to make it happen. This was the right forum for Cheryl to introduce her vision, which the team then embraced. Their main concern – particularly as operators – would be the challenge of translating rhetoric into action. One of Cheryl's core strengths was execution, hence her rapid rise into the directorship role, and she was able to lead the team in putting in place a measurable plan with various workstreams focused on engagement, growth, efficiencies and sustainability.

Cheryl followed up with personal one-to-one conversations to ensure each team member felt fully heard, understood and supported. She asked for help in taking ownership of the plan and requested feedback about how she was leading the operation to quickly course-correct. The team went out to the factory and conducted listening groups to share the direction of travel and get the necessary insight to ensure things were done in the right way. Engagement levels went up, changes were made, and the operation went on to function in better and more efficient ways.

What is the meaning that you have given your work? Have you reflected upon it long enough to have derived a meaning that nourishes and sustains you? Here are seven statements we use to help define the meaning of work:

Work is a form of service helping the world to become a better place.

Work is a way to express your creativity and to make your mark.

Work is an opportunity to connect with others and to build rewarding relationships.

> Work allows you to accelerate your learning and development to become a better version of you.

> Work provides reward and remuneration in the form of recognition and money.

> Work fulfils personal and organizational purpose, giving direction and inspiration.

> Work makes life worthwhile by meeting the fundamental human needs of security, belonging, esteem and self-actualization.

For those leading and supporting others, one of the most meaningful work contributions you can make is to help others find the work they love. Graham Alexander, Founder of The Alexander Partnership, shared his wisdom on the matter:

As a leader or manager, explore what your people would love to do and help them discover a role they would love. This is diametrically opposed to the normal approach that most organizations take of finding people to fit roles. People appear to be motivated by one primary driver, which, once you understand what it is, puts you in a position to help them align it with their work. This combination makes a big difference to enabling people to do the work they love.

He encourages people to look through four lenses to understand their primary motivation:

1 **Intrinsic reward** – where primary motivation is connected with inner feelings such as feeling valued, enjoying what you do and gaining satisfaction from your work
2 **Extrinsic reward** – where primary motivation is driven by external factors including the desire for status, fame, recognition and remuneration
3 **Relationship** – where primary motivation is relational, such as being part of a team and collaborating with others.
4 **World** – where primary motivation is linked with helping to create a better world and doing meaningful work that makes a tangible difference to others.

Graham Alexander went on to say: 'Be known for helping people love their work. This is a gap in most organizational and leadership approaches which prioritizes roles over people loving what they do.' We recognize that making meaning is not a one-off job. It's a daily process to pay attention and be intentional about the meaning you want to bring to work, translating what happens in the workplace in meaningful ways and helping others do meaningful work.

♥ Lovenote

To make work more meaningful, consider three questions:
• Does what you do really matter?
• Is it something that has not been done before?
• Will it make a significant difference to others?

Believe it's possible

What if the point of work was to help the next generation be better equipped to solve their problems and make the world a better place? What if your work was dedicated to making your version of Steve Jobs's sentiment 'Make a dent in the universe'? We recognize the essential needs for money and security, but even within the context of meeting basic requirements there is opportunity to contribute in ways that inspire you and others.

We resonate wholeheartedly with the way Renée Elliott, founder of Planet Organic and co-founder of Beluga Bean, expressed this in our interview:

> I see life [as having] three stages – Learn, Earn and Return. My life now is about guiding the next generation through the pitfalls of running a business and learning from the mistakes I made. There is no doubt that if I knew then what I know now, it would have been a different game. I feel strongly about being a caretaker to nurture others. I believe in the importance of elders and mentoring others. I realize that people need life skills to navigate through business, as a lot of what you need in work you don't learn at school and in the family.

Wim Dejonghe, Senior Partner at Allen & Overy, put it succinctly when we asked him for his advice about making a difference through work: 'Have pride in what you build. It's important to leave things in a better place and ready for the next generation.' We also appreciated the sentiment from Staynton Brown, Director Diversity and Inclusion and Talent at Transport for London, who reflected upon the future in light of the pandemic:

> COVID-19 has led to people doing some amazing things. It's helped develop connections and solidarity. For instance, people have had the time to build relationships rather than just keeping busy. We have seen so many examples of people doing small things that have added real value – from collecting packages for neighbours through to clapping for our carers. We now need to bring these acts into our normal life as it gives people nourishment and soul food.

How can you make your work soul food? Latifah worked in cybersecurity for a global bank. It was hard to see how her work could nourish her soul! Normal days consisted of relentless back-to-back meetings, hitting Asia in the morning and America in the afternoon, with Europe sandwiched in the middle. When we met with Latifah and she tried to explain the complexity and challenge of mitigating sophisticated fraud, we found it mind-boggling. There didn't seem to be any room for soul food, and yet Latifah knew that her work had to contribute more than saving the bank money.

We entered into deep and meaningful conversations about her future and what Latifah wanted to create. It was clear that her role in cybersecurity was a vehicle to fulfil a bigger picture focused on helping others love their work. From an early age Latifah had an intuitive belief that it was possible to do what you love and love what you do, but she hadn't had any role models to show her the way. One of Latifah's primary strengths lay in simplifying complexity, which she put to good use in navigating the murky world of fraud. However, her other strengths lay in leading and developing others, which she was now keen to tap into.

We introduced her to the work of Richard Boyatzis, Distinguished University Professor of Organizational Behavior, Psychology, and Cognitive Science at Case Western Reserve University, whose book *Helping People Change* provides a science-based answer to that all-important question 'How can I help?'. In our interview with Richard, he shared his theory that 'To create sustainable change, it's vital to develop a personal vision consisting of your ideal self which becomes a driver of hope. Once you have this in place, it gives you a chance of experiencing sustainable learning and change.' He continued:

> In terms of a relationship, team, organization, country and even global processes ... developing a shared vision and passion is probably the most powerful predictor of engagement, organizational citizenship, effectiveness in role and innovation. The distinction is that you need to have a dream and a sense of possibility that drive you rather than a commitment to a goal. Having goals is useful, which play a part in creating the future. However, if you focus on the goal too quickly, you activate a part of your brain known as the task-positive network (TPN) which closes you down to new ideas, and as a consequence you literally squelch the durability of your effort.

Latifah was hooked. She focused on developing her vision, of which a large element was about helping others in the field of work. This included mentoring young people in discovering the work they would love to do, developing her team members to progress in meaningful ways and taking an active role in supporting a Women in Leadership initiative. Inspired by her vision, Latifah showed up for work in a different way. She no longer saw it as primarily a transaction to reach specific metrics, but as a means to progressing the causes closest to her heart. Latifah was energized and excited by this broader perspective, and started to look forward to each day as an opportunity to build momentum around her own agenda. Latifah's future took on a very different shape. No longer boxed in by her role, she developed her ability in multiple ways. She commented:

> I had never really thought about the breadth of opportunities that could be linked to work. I grew up with such a narrow view that had caused me to pursue a singular route. Now I feel passionate about and contribute to a balanced suite of projects, all of which adds to making work something I love.

The starting point to shaping the future is to conduct a situational analysis about where you are today so that you have an honest picture about your current state. Will had just landed a new dream role. However, when he came to us for coaching, he was wracked with insecurity. He had been made redundant from his last three roles for various reasons including being in the wrong role, failing to navigate internal politics and the company getting sold. During this time Will had experienced a panic attack during a particularly stressful period, and this had dented his confidence for engaging in high-profile meetings and presenting. He was afraid that he would underperform in his new role and that this would diminish his future prospects.

We sat down with Will to understand his current reality. We looked at all angles including personal factors such as family, health and finance as well as professional influences such as capability, knowledge and stakeholder relationships. It transpired that on the work side Will was in a genuinely good place. He had been successful in a rigorous interview and assessment process, and early on in his new role had reached out to his line manager for feedback, receiving reassurance that he was on track.

It was a different story on the personal side, however. Will's father, with whom he had a distant relationship at the best of times, was in poor health. As a father himself, Will was now encountering difficulties with his own teenage son who was spending the majority of his time gaming. Will was closer to his mother but had not shared the full picture of his life with her, and he had little contact with his brother who was struggling with addiction. Will had a loving relationship with his wife but recognized that, given his work schedule, he left the majority of parenting to her and failed to provide sufficient support even when he was around. His health was in a good place and he had achieved a high level of performance in a particular sport. From a financial position, Will was very driven to achieve security. He was on track, but suffered anxiety worrying about whether the money would keep coming in.

Having got a good picture of his current situation, we asked Will about his future vision. Although he could articulate a high-level description of his desired future, Will needed to give more in-depth thought to activate his Positive Emotional Attractor (see Chapter 2), which would lead to sustained change. We shared with him the work of Richard Boyatzis, who emphasizes the importance of clarifying a person's dreams and aspirations aligned with their core identity, values and purpose.

Will dived into his vision with the dynamic drive which helped him to be successful in his work. He spent time with his wife exploring it and incorporated their shared dreams. From this place of vision he was motivated to resolve some of the outstanding issues in his personal world. He reached out to his parents and was able to share his love and appreciation as well as reaching for a new level of honesty regarding his own struggles, which previously he had largely hidden from them. They were very supportive and grateful for his openness and willingness to engage. Will also reconnected with his brother, which at first proved very challenging as there was sibling conflict, as well as his brother's instability, to navigate. However, they agreed to reset their relationship and see how they could have a more meaningful connection going forward. Possibly most importantly, Will made important decisions about his own parenting. He decided to stop reacting to his son and to extend empathy and acceptance in order to get into his world. Over time, the walls came down and they reconnected in a way that led to a healthier father–son partnership. Rebuilding his foundation from a personal perspective unleashed Will's energy for work, and he was able to help accelerate the company growth and create a better tomorrow.

Shaping the future as you would like it to be lies in your hands and requires you to go deeper into the discovery of yourself. As Kai Reinhardt, Professor of Digital Management, Organization and HR at the University of Technology and Economics Berlin, shared in our interview:

> Stay authentic to avoid stepping into a role stereotype. This is the only chance you have. If you try to force yourself into a role that is not you, it won't work in the volatile dynamics that we are navigating today. Be yourself and allow your skills to come through. If you are the introverted thinker in the corner, be the introvert in the corner and use your analytical skills. If you are the extrovert who needs to jump into difficult situations, then do so and show your expertise. It's interesting to note that in Germany, for example, we used to make a cultural distinction between the formal and informal self, according to expected management thinking. Now, working in multiple networks, the formal self is redundant. There is no form of distance anymore. It makes no sense to have a formal distance between the person and the role. I encourage people to make the statement, 'I love my passion and I am me.'

Laura Miller, Executive Vice President, Chief Information Officer, at Macy's, put it this way:

> Don't take yourself so seriously. Enjoy the journey more. Growing up as a female in an engineering environment there was a lot of competition. I felt that I had to be better than my peers, work more hours and prove myself. However, I don't know if it really paid off! Part of loving what you do is having the balance between your personal life as much as your work. I realize that I took myself too seriously and over-indexed on work. If I could do it again, I would go back and balance it out more.

A powerful process for shaping the future as you would like it to be is known as the 'rocking chair test'. Fast-forward to the end of your life. See yourself sitting by a cosy log fire in a beautiful room surrounded by those people who meant the most to you in your life, work and community. Everyone is here to reflect on the life you lived, the relationships you built, the work you did and the difference you made in the world. You get to nominate whom you want to speak and ask to share their experience of you. Maybe you have a partner whom you ask to share the impact you had in your relationship. For those with children, maybe they will describe what it was like to be parented by you. You might have wider family members who will talk about the qualities you embodied. From a work perspective you could ask past managers, colleagues, customers and influencers to discuss the difference you made through your work and what drove you. In terms of community, you could invite some special people who were close to the contribution you made as a global citizen.

As you sit in your rocking chair, you make a note of everything you hear. This is recorded indelibly in your mind's eye. It resonates wholeheartedly with what you believe, with what you love and with how you want to be. It is a future that energizes and inspires you. It is a future which provides the reason for loving your work. You make a decision – wherever you are and whatever is going on today you will take a stand for loving what you do and doing what you love. You believe in this possibility. Even if you feel a mile away right now, it simply fills you with more drive to turn the dream into a reality. You commit to discovering and following your purpose; being inspired by a compelling vision; living your values; playing to your strengths; building great relationships; accelerating your learning; adapting your approach and making a difference. You have the framework to love your work. See yourself getting up from your rocking chair, thanking everyone for their insight, and making a public declaration about your intent to learn, grow and elevate your work to new heights – *starting now*.

Remember that the skill and art of doing the work you love lie in your hands. No one can do it for you. People can guide you and open up opportunities, but it's you who needs to shape and drive your work so that it becomes a catalyst for realizing your dreams and touching the lives of others in meaningful ways.

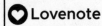 **Lovenote**

Loving what you do more and doing what you love more often starts with the belief that it's possible.

At the heart of it

Don't wait to make work matter.

Every day you have the opportunity to make work matter for you, for others and for the world around you.

What effect are you having?

Choose what impact you want to have.
Stretch your capacity and capability to do more.
Do what matters most.

Make work meaningful. Make memories you feel proud of.
Make it your life's work.

Reprise

As we reach the end of our journey together in this book, let's pause and reflect on how you are feeling about your relationship with the work you do. Can you see the path forward to recover your affection for where you work, or discover the determination to shape your work to make it better?

Before you move into the implementation phase to make great things happen in your work life, let's recap on the three key stages we've identified together:

Stage 1: Discover where we explored finding your fuel, opening your mind and unlocking your code to set your personal foundations for future success.

Stage 2: Develop where we looked at activating momentum, 'giving and getting' in relationships at work, and accelerating evolution to move things forward at pace.

Stage 3: Deliver where we focused on making it matter and the real difference you can achieve.

Here's a quick whistle-stop reminder of the seven steps behind those stages which will help you not just survive but truly thrive at work:

7.
MAKE IT MATTER

Have pride in what you build. Make an impact. Make a meaningful difference. Make a positive change to create long-lasting love for your work.

6.
ACCELERATE EVOLUTION

Learn to love change and you will love work more. Be constantly curious about the benefits of change, iteration and improvement, and do not just accept but accelerate evolution.

5.
GIVE AND GET

To thrive at work, invest smartly in your relationships. Your emotional 'bank accounts' with others need continuous, skilled management.

4.
ACTIVATE MOMENTUM

Play to your strengths, unlock your potential, get in flow and aim for progress over perfection – these actions will give you the firepower for acceleration.

3.
UNLOCK YOUR CODE

Think of this as a treasure hunt, with your values, decision-making criteria and framework as powerful clues, helping you on the adventure towards doing what you love.

2.
OPEN YOUR MIND

If you want to love what you do, you need to do what inspires you.

1.
FIND YOUR FUEL

The most important factor to doing what you love and loving what you do is to understand your own purpose and to let it fuel your work.

The 3D LoveWork Model™

1 Find your fuel

For motivation and momentum and for the energy and enjoyment of work, we need to start with what fuels us – our purpose.

Richard Solomons, Chairman of Rentokil, shares the impact that thinking deeply and acting deliberately 'on purpose' had on him:

> What helped unlock my paradigm about work was focusing on my purpose, which has its roots in creating opportunity. By thinking proactively about what I am doing, why I am doing it and being deliberate about where I spend my time it has had a big impact on deriving fulfilment from my work.

Amy Edmondson, Novartis Professor of Leadership and Management at Harvard Business School, sums up the fundamentals:

> Doing the work you love starts with purpose and having something you care about. Look for something that matters, for example improving health or creating a beautiful space to live and work in. Name what speaks to you. Find a worthy cause because you are going to spend the dominant hours of your life on it.

Finding your fuel is critical but not always easy. It is also inherently individual; your purpose is completely personal. Like any relationships, with work it's about getting the right match. Professor Amy Edmondson reminds us of this with her simple exhortation: 'Make sure you love what you do. For instance, if you hate writing, don't become an academic! If you don't like working with your hands, don't become a carpenter.'

We believe that when you do love your work, it can be transformative. Khaled Ismail, Vice President Communications, Europe, Central Asia, Middle East and Africa, at Tetra Pak, sums up the perfect formula and the effect of doing what you love: 'Loving my work means bringing together the enjoyment of what I do alongside working with good human beings. I am thankful that I love what I do with people I enjoy working with. What more can I ask for?'

The reality of work for many people is so often focused away from this. We are aiming towards another person's concept of success or we see work as fundamentally something to be endured, not enjoyed. Stephen McCall, Chief Executive Officer at edyn, shares his story:

> In my own journey of work I initially didn't have a clear view on purpose. My priority was about position as I got wrapped up in securing bigger roles, more money and higher status. It was at a time in the 1990s when there wasn't a lot of thought given to purpose. I had also been brought up to believe that work was hard and that you had to suffer through it. I had no concept that work could be about enjoyment.

He goes on to articulate one of the reasons we felt the need to write this book:

> I believe that one of the biggest tragedies in life is people spending a large amount of time in abject misery. It can't be the right thing to do. We need to apply a more sophisticated thought process about work and not leave it until later in life. I do see the next generation questioning 'Why work?'. I often see Gen X, Y and Zs perceived as being entitled. It's not true. They are asking the questions previous generations should have asked. For instance, if it's true to say that everyone has a purpose, and that you won't be fulfilled until you are following it, then if your purpose and work are incompatible, you will be miserable.

We love the way Renée Elliott, founder of Planet Organic and co-founder of Beluga Bean, articulates her approach: 'I am a great believer in knowing your passions, interests, and realizing what you are here to do. I believe we are born with a purpose. I used to whisper to my children, "Remember why you came", in order to help them unlock their potential.'

'Remember why you came' and 'Do what you love'. Know your purpose and understand why you do what you do. The clearer you are about your raison d'être – your reason for being – the more your work will be an expression of it. Power a greater, better, happier life at work by allowing yourself the time to find what fuels your sense of fulfilment and enjoyment.

2 Open your mind

We wouldn't be surprised if this was the hardest chapter in the book or the most difficult step to think through for you. With those we work with, pausing judgement, suspending conditioning and silencing the internal critics and opinionated voices in order to open up your mind is a challenging process. But when you are willing to explore all possibilities, great things can happen.

In order to do inspired work, you need to be inspired. To find the sparks that will ignite your inspiration, prioritize being open to new experiences. Make sure you have access to inspiring role models who lift you up and help you to see things differently. Both of us personally have a broad range of mentors whom we draw upon to inspire us across all areas of our work, life and relationships. Challenge your status quo by being prepared to question your assumptions about how you think things 'have' to be. For instance, one of the potential benefits coming out of the COVID-19 crisis is a new level of flexibility for how we work. Organizations are encouraging people to be performance-oriented and put the objective of their work ahead of *where* they work. The old assumption that you have to put in a long commute to work in a single office to do multiple types of work is over.

Committing your work to be an expression of your vision will amplify the positivity of your relationship with it. In *Helping People Change*, you may remember, authors Richard Boyatzis, Melvin Smith and Ellen Van Oosten show how asking yourself thought-provoking questions awakens your Positive Emotional Attractor, which activates parts of the brain that trigger hormones – the parasympathetic nervous system – associated with emotions such as awe, joy, gratitude and curiosity. The big question to explore is: 'If my work life were ideal ten to fifteen years from now, what would it be like?'

It's critical to allow your brain to be open to possibility and to let your mind imagine where your work could go. Consider the idea that you could love your work, and with regular practice you can get there. We have seen that big results come from small actions, regularly practised. *Atomic Habits* author James Clear shows how to change your habits and get 1 per cent better every day, recommending the technique of asking daily questions to reflect, review and keep your mind working around what's possible.

Applying this technique is a powerful way of becoming better at opening your mind on a consistent basis. It will lift you up. It will help you be inspired, and this will help you to do inspired work. It can also connect you with the unknown – what inspires you may be something you haven't yet realized.

3 Unlock your code

Your individual 'code' is shaped by your own experiences. This code gives you a framework of values which help simplify and inform what is most important to you. Following this intentionally and thoughtfully will mean you make decisions that amplify the potential of you finding true love for your work and creating the conditions for you to flourish.

Staynton Brown, Director Diversity and Inclusion and Talent, Transport for London, described how his life experiences shaped his values in a way which has deeply impacted his work:

> I was the eldest of four, raised by my mum who worked three jobs and who ensured we grew up in a loving family. I developed a sense of responsibility from an early age which drove my work ethic and determination to do something bigger than myself. Being black has had a bearing. Particularly as a child I was told that I would have to work harder, and that discrimination and barriers did exist. At an early age I realized the unfairness of the social model of inequality and wanted to challenge it. I have read multiple works from diverse thinkers which triggered my ambition to be a polymath. I love bringing lots of different ideas and disciplines to situations. From a professional standpoint I have worked in the justice sector, education, public health and now with a local government body. During this time I have had the opportunity to work with amazing people who have been generous with their time and experience and this has fuelled my passion for diversity and inclusion.

Acting in a way which is 'against your code' creates a dissonance which makes you uncomfortable and unhappy in the workplace. Conversely, creating a framework based around your values and acting in a way which is in line with this code will dramatically increase your ability to feel good about your work.

Sonja Vodusek is the Managing Director for the legendary hotel The Peninsula in London and an example of someone who intentionally acts in line with her code. Before leaving for London, she was General Manager of The Peninsula in Tokyo. Her team encouraged her to put on a big leaving celebration, but as the timing was in the middle of the Rugby World Cup, she refused as she didn't want to create additional work. However, guided by one of her core values of 'being approachable', she instead set up an open house where anyone at any level could come and have a conversation with her. Thinking there would be limited take-up, she scheduled three three-hour sessions on consecutive days. Colleagues queued around the hotel corridors to have a chat. Some wanted to talk about their career development and get feedback. Others brought family members. She had to keep scheduling more and more time to ensure everyone had a chance to chat.

As a leader, Sonja hires people on values, not skills. This increasingly common approach in organizations makes it more important than ever to be crystal clear on your 'code' – know your values and you'll know where your values will fit. Hold true to that code to energize and strengthen the chances of doing the work you love.

4 Activate momentum

Our first three steps took us on a journey to discover firm personal foundations for success by defining what fuels us, opening minds to being inspired and clarifying the code by which we want to operate. Building on those firm foundations moves us into the development stage of *LoveWork*, so that we can activate the momentum needed to move forward at pace, and sustain and energize our relationship with work.

This starts with playing to your individual strengths to increase the impact you can have, from the first impressions you make, through to the transformation of businesses and teams, right through to your lifetime legacy.

You do also need to tenaciously identify and remove the barriers that could get in the way of fulfilling your potential. Amy Edmondson, Novartis Professor of Leadership and Management at Harvard Business School, talked about the need to overcome the barrier of fear to do what you love:

> I believe that fear and love are at odds. Even in a relationship it's hard to experience love when you are afraid. Fear can run the spectrum from being terrified to low-level anxiety, but wherever you are on the spectrum it will block you from feeling truly engaged and loving what you do. Sometimes the fear is within you. For instance, you might be unconsciously bringing in learned fear from a past experience, or the fear can be the result of a manager or organization. Whatever the source, it's important to recognize the fear and move beyond it by believing that it is possible to do what you love.

Wim Dejonghe, Senior Partner, Allen & Overy, described how early life experiences helped him overcome blockers, which contributed to his future work:

> I wasn't raised in an environment that caused me to believe that I would get what I wanted so when opportunities came my way it was a nice surprise. For instance, I became the manager of the sailing school where I taught and then I secured the role of a research assistant at university without having the perfect skillset. My first job offer at a law firm was a bigger opportunity than I thought was possible. These experiences led me to realize I could add value which became part of my identity and ultimately helped me to develop leadership skills.

If you can consciously and repeatedly find opportunities to allow you to focus on being in flow — that glorious state of concentration or deep enjoyment — you will continue to expand yourself in a way which is thrilling and fulfilling. The choice you then need to make is to actively keep moving forward, choosing progress over perfection, so that the constant incremental gains lead to exponential growth for you and for any teams you are part of. We are iterative beings and can always become better versions of ourselves. By activating momentum you keep moving forward to learn, grow and develop.

5 Give and get

It's not (all) about you. Work fulfilment is developed by building great relationships, partnerships and making a big difference in others' lives. Angela Brav, President Hertz International, is clear about this:

> Work provides me with a sense of purpose through transforming other people's lives. It enables me to connect with others. Work is an opportunity to provide fulfilment and meaning through making a difference in people's lives, whether it is colleagues, customers, consumers or the community.

This sentiment is echoed by David Woodward, former CEO Heinz Europe,

> When we help people achieve what they didn't think they were capable of, it is hugely rewarding. For instance, I know people who have had significant limitations, but by majoring on their strengths and having the right people around them have gone on to excel.

Staynton Brown, Director Diversity and Inclusion and Talent at Transport for London, sums this up brilliantly:

> In Francis Bacon's essay 'Of Friendship', he states: 'Whosoever is delighted in solitude is either a wild beast or a god.' We can't get away from the fact that we are social animals. We need interaction and human connection. Developing relationships is a vital ingredient of work so make sure that you invest in them in fair and just ways.

Work is an amazing vehicle to build lifelong partnerships with amazing people. Some of our clients go back over 25 years, and we've worked together through life transformations and sweeping changes in history. We have had the good fortune to partner with people through multiple organizations, helping them navigate the ups and downs of the business world. The majority of our work comes through personal connections and enduring partnerships that help promote what we do across the world. As we look back on our work, the most meaningful elements are the relationships we have built, and as we look forward, what excites us is the opportunity to develop more partnerships, particularly with a concept like *LoveWork* to fuel creativity and explore possibilities with others.

Give and get is based on trust as that is the glue that makes relationships stick. Start from a place of trusting others until proved otherwise. Be clear about how you demonstrate trust, and instigate transparent conversations with people you work with about how to get the best out of each other. Prioritize diversity and inclusion in your partnerships.

What's changed significantly in the last few years is the understanding that working with people 'like you' is not necessarily the right strategy for the long-term good of either the business or your personal growth. Deliberately choose people to work with who are different from you. Recognize that bias is a natural condition. You will never rid yourself of it, but it is a lifelong challenge to keep increasing your awareness of bias and to become more inclusive.

We will always need to deliver our work to a range of different people. Being prepared to forge relationships with those who think and work in diverse ways will strengthen your empathy and connection skills. It's part of your ability to learn and grow which is fulfilling – and will help you flourish. As Nick Dent, Director of Customer Operations, London Underground, put it: 'I love the social interaction and buzz of meeting different people, exploring different perspectives and how work enriches my life overall. What I've learned at work has helped me have better conversations with my family and friends.'

We can get so much from others but we need to give to them, too – to believe in them and be ready to share our stories. Nurture high engagement and collaboration through authentic storytelling, bringing others into your world and finding where you have common ground for doing the work you love.

6 Accelerate evolution

It has only been since around 2010 that the powerful tools of cognitive neuroscience have been applied to understanding insight. Tools such as the electroencephalogram (EEG) and functional magnetic resonance imaging (fMRI) are being used to unravel the neural mechanisms that underlie creative insights. Have you had the experience of that 'aha!' or 'eureka!' moment that gives you the momentum to make progress? This insight is learning in action stimulated by curiosity. Be a lifelong learner. Prioritize learning. Seek learning. Welcome learning. Stay curious, always.

In the wake of the global COVID-19 pandemic, never have we required higher degrees of 'agility ability' to sprint forwards into a new world of flexibility and dynamic working. John Holland-Kaye, CEO at Heathrow, shared his perspective on how his learning agility accelerated his evolution:

> The first job I had was in strategy consulting where the most valued prize was intellect. I realized that I wasn't the smartest in the room. However, later in my career I recognized that I didn't need to be. I went into industry sectors where I was not an expert and was forced to speed up my learning by asking multiple questions and drawing logical conclusions. I had people working for me who had numerous years of experience and found that we could combine our strengths of strategy and delivery to good effect.

One of John's colleagues, Jonathan Coen, Director of Security, discussed the significant role learning has played in his evolution:

> It took me some time to learn how to separate between developing technical competencies like writing a strategy paper and learning through others' ideas. For instance, I have built a team who are committed to challenging the status quo with different ideas and who are prepared to listen and learn. This plays into my purpose about unlocking the art of the possible and to being as creative as possible.

Given the explosion of technology in the world of work, it was valuable to understand the point of view of Kai Reinhardt, Professor of Digital Management, Organization and HR at the University of Technology and Economics Berlin:

> Technology can speed up the process from translating ideas to execution. Find out what speeds up your personal creation process. I wouldn't recommend one tool. You have to mesh everything together. It's no longer a binary world like using Microsoft or Apple. It's everything. Every tool has a benefit. You need to use the tools that have the maximum impact for the situation you're in. Grab what's useful. Don't stick to the tools you have used in the past. Technology can improve, but you have to accept that it is overwhelming as well. What makes it easier is when you come across tools that deliver a great user experience which makes work easier and more effective.

Amy Edmondson, Novartis Professor of Leadership and Management at Harvard Business School, endorsed the need to constantly evolve:

> Loving your work is not the same as having a great time at a party. Work needs to be a stretch. If work does not challenge us, then it is not going to have the satisfaction we are seeking. If we are not learning, growing and being stretched in some way, then we are starting a process of giving up. Stretch looks different for everyone. For instance, what could look like a wild risk to the majority of people is a viable proposition for an entrepreneur. Successful entrepreneurs take the right level of risk for themselves. It is within their bounds, however their tolerance for uncertainty and failure is greater than the majority, which is why they become entrepreneurs.

Be deliberate about building stretch, challenge, learning and growth into your work. This will ensure that whatever is going on with your work, you will benefit. At times of adversity, ambiguity and setbacks, understanding that you can bounce back in a better place is a source of resilience. At times of flow and success, avoiding any complacency by challenging yourself to be a better version of yourself and do better work will keep you on track. It's within your power to evolve ... fast.

7 Make it matter

Now that we have covered the Discover and Develop stages of *Love-Work*, the final stage is Deliver – making things happen that make it all matter. Probably one of the most frequent feelings we hear from people is that they want to make a difference. This needs to be followed up with the critical, deeper inquiry into what type of difference it is that you want to make in 'making the hours count' rather than just counting the hours at work.

Angela Brav, President of Hertz International, shared her perspective:

> In one role I led a function that had a pattern of underperformance. Over the next few years I deliberately made very few lay-offs. People stopped worrying about losing their jobs and we focused on developing systems to hit our numbers every year. Since then my goal has been to create organizations where people come to work because they believe in you and the company. I have focused on achieving higher goals and creating environments where people can be at their best and deliver amazing results.

Back to John Holland-Kaye, CEO at Heathrow, who balances the need to run a business, satisfy multiple stakeholder agendas and fulfil his commitment to making a difference:

> Your legacy lies in the people you have worked with and what they have gained from working with you and how it's helped them go on to better things. What gives me the greatest satisfaction is seeing people developing their careers and doing the work they love.

Be clear about the type of difference you want to make. Ask yourself: 'What value do I want to add in my work?' And 'How will I know that I have made a lasting and meaningful difference through my work?' There is no greater gift than doing the work you love and loving the work you do that makes a positive difference in others' lives.

Epilogue

We are reaching the end of this book, but if our work has had the impact we intend, this will mark the start of something new, exciting, enriching and enlivening for you and your work.

We have worked with and spoken to a wide variety of people who have shaped their life so that they can fill it with moments where they love what they do. Believe that this is possible for you, too. Recognize that, with analysis, thought and intentional action, you can find greater fulfilment and enjoyment in your work.

Our hope is that *LoveWork* gives you the framework, ideas and confidence to do the work you love and love the work you do. By applying the principles and tools in the book you will discover a new meaning in work that will help you thrive, engage others along the way and help make the world a better place.

Our aim in this guide is to help you achieve this, but, of course, the only way for it to have real impact is dependent on you making an important decision – to take time to consciously understand yourself and to actively build a positive work relationship. There is the old cliché often given in relationship breakdowns, 'It's not you, it's me.' In work relationships, we often see that it's not always the work itself that needs to reset, it can be you. The truth is that a successful relationship with work is all about you being clear what you want and understanding what it is that makes you feel good and do well. Self-knowledge is a critical goal, but we are very clear that it is a challenging one to work towards. As Benjamin Franklin expressed it, back in the eighteenth century: 'There are three things extremely hard: steel, a diamond, and to know one's self.'

Like real-life romantic love stories, work stories are complex. The dream of a 'happy ending' in relationships or the 'perfect work–life' balance is, of course, dangerous because perfection in relationships is impossible, and inevitably all work will be tiring, difficult or complicated at times. And the idea of 'following your passion' in both can be misleading. We know there will always be tough times and difficult Mondays, but by taking time to work through these key steps you can find a path to make sure that work is not something that must be endured but something that can be enjoyed. The thrill of acting on purpose, being inspired and navigating around your own code cannot be underestimated. Moving with momentum, building relationships and making things evolve faster leads to great pace and progress. Making it matter means that work can be a great part of your one precious life.

The language of salaries as 'compensation' always feels interesting as it implies we must be compensated for the challenges of the workplace. We are practical people. We know that the choices we make about what work we do are influenced by myriad financial, geographic or socio-economic factors. This book is not a blanket 'follow your dreams' but a pragmatic guide to making the most of what is within your smart, personal control. It's about making considered choices and understanding the behavioural science and psychology behind what you can do to flourish and feel fulfilled. And it's about believing it's possible to take action to shape and develop a bigger, better, bolder way of working with more meaning.

Our *cri de cœur* as we finish this book is for you to use it as the starting point for making great things happen. Let us know how you get on. Share your stories with us (and find out more) at golovework.com, follow us on Instagram and Twitter @golovework and connect with us both on LinkedIn. We'd love to hear your thoughts. And we'd love you to fill your days with more of what you can love.

Love work!

References

Ackerman, Courtney E., 'What is neuroplasticity? A psychologist explains'. Positive Psychology, 2 May 2021, available at https://positivepsychology.com/neuroplasticity/.

Boyatzis, Richard, Smith, Melvin and Van Oosten, Ellen, *Helping People Change*. Harvard Business Review Press, 2019.

Brown, Brené, *Daring Greatly*. Penguin Books, 2015.

Brown, Steven, Major-Girardin, Judy and Yuan, Ye, 'Storytelling Is Intrinsically Mentalistic: A Functional Magnetic Resonance Imaging Study of Narrative Production across Modalities'. *Journal of Cognitive Neuroscience*, vol. 30, no. 9, September 2018, available at https://direct.mit.edu/jocn/article/30/9/1298/28916/Storytelling-Is-Intrinsically-Mentalistic-A.

Bradberry, Travis, 'Why you need emotional intelligence to succeed'. *Forbes*, 7 January 2015, available at https://www.forbes.com/sites/travisbradberry/2015/01/07/why-you-need-emotional-intelligence-to-succeed/?sh=6922fb862468.

Buckingham, Marcus and Goodall, Ashley, *Nine Lies About Work*. Harvard Business Review Press, 2019.

Campbell, Celeste, 'What is neuroplasticity?' Brainline, 4 February 2009, available at https://www.brainline.org/author/celeste-campbell/qa/what-neuroplasticity.

Carlsson-Szlezak, Philipp, Reeves, Martin and Swartz, Paul, 'Understanding the Economic Shock of Coronavirus'. Harvard Business Review, 27 March 2020, available at https://hbr.org/2020/03/understanding-the-economic-shock-of-coronavirus.

Clear, James, *Atomic Habits*. Random House Business, 2018.

Cranston, Susie and Keller, Scott, 'Increasing the "meaning quotient" of work'. *McKinsey Quarterly*, 1 January 2013, available at https://www.mckinsey.com/business-functions/organization/our-insights/increasing-the-meaning-quotient-of-work.

Csikszentmihalyi, Mihaly, *Flow: The Psychology of Optimal Experience.* Harper Perennial Modern Classics, 1990.

Dewar, Carolyn, Keller, Scott, Sneader, Kevin and Strovink, Kurt, 'The CEO moment: Leadership for a new era'. *McKinsey Quarterly*, 21 July 2020, available at https://www.mckinsey.com/featured-insights/leadership/the-ceo-moment-leadership-for-a-new-era.

Dweck, Carol, *Mindset*. Robinson, 2012.

Eger, Edith, *The Choice*. Rider Books, 2018.

Elkins, Kathleen, 'Bill Gates says he retired from Microsoft nearly a decade earlier than he intended—here's why'. CNBC, 2019, available at https://www.cnbc.com/2019/09/26/bill-gates-the-day-i-knew-what-i-wanted-to-do-for-the-rest-of-my-life.html.

Gates, Bill, *The Road Ahead*. Viking, 1995.

Gavett, Gretchen, 'Do we really need the office?' *Harvard Business Review*, 15 July 2020, available at https://hbr.org/2020/07/do-we-really-need-the-office.

Ginsberg, Leah, 'The one book that changed Oprah Winfrey's life and business'. CNBC, 17 June 2017, available at https://www.cnbc.com/2017/06/15/the-one-book-that-changed-oprah-winfreys-life-and-business.html.

Goleman, Daniel, *Emotional Intelligence: Why It Can Matter More Than IQ* Bloomsbury Publishing, 1996.

Google Project Aristotle, re:Work. Google, available at https://rework.withgoogle.com/guides/understanding-team-effectiveness/steps/introduction/.

Hope, Daniel, 'My mentor Yehudi Menuhin: "I can still hear his beautiful sound"', *The Guardian*, 29 March 2016, available at https://www.theguardian.com/music/2016/mar/29/yehudi-menuhin-by-daniel-hope-violinist.

HM Government, 'Analysis of the health, economic and social effects of COVID-19 and the approach to tiering', 30 November 2020, available at https://assets.publishing.service.gov.uk/government/uploads/system/uploads/attachment_data/file/944823/Analysis_of_the_health_economic_and_social_effects_of_COVID-19_and_the_approach_to_tiering_FINAL_-_accessible_v2.pdf.

Isaacson, Walter, *Steve Jobs*. Little, Brown, 2011.

Kahneman, Daniel, *Thinking, Fast and Slow*. Penguin Books, 2012.

Kashdan, Todd, 'Wired to wonder'. *Greater Good Magazine*, 1 September 2009, available at https://greatergood.berkeley.edu/article/item/wired_to_wonder.

Kaufman, Scott Barry, 'Why inspiration matters'. *Psychology Today*, 5 October 2011, available at https://www.psychologytoday.com/gb/blog/beautiful-minds/201110/why-inspiration-matters.

Korn Ferry, 'Self-Disrupt or Be Disrupted', 2019, available at https://www.kornferry.com/insights/featured-topics/leadership/self-disruptive-leader.

Law, Tara, '"Superforecasters" Are Making Eerily Accurate Predictions About COVID-19. Our Leaders Could Learn From

Their Approach'. *TIME*, 11 June 2020, available at https://time.com/5848271/superforecasters-covid-19/.

Robinson, Ken, 'Do schools kill creativity?' *TED: Ideas Worth Spreading*, February 2006, available at https://www.ted.com/talks/sir_ken_robinson_do_schools_kill_creativity/transcript?language=en.

Swart, Tara, 'The 4 underlying principles of changing your brain'. *Forbes*, 27 March 2018, available at https://www.forbes.com/sites/taraswart/2018/03/27/the-4-underlying-principles-to-changing-your-brain/?sh=30eef4215a71.

Trench, Sally, *Bury Me in My Boots*. Hodder & Stoughton, 1968.

Ware, Bronnie, *The Top Five Regrets of the Dying*. Hay House, 2012.

Webber, Alan M., 'What's so new about the new economy?' *Harvard Business Review*, January–February 1993, available at https://hbr.org/1993/01/whats-so-new-about-the-new-economy.

World Health Organization, 'Mental Health & COVID-19', WHO, 2020, available at https://www.who.int/teams/mental-health-and-substance-use/covid-19.

Winfrey, Oprah, *The Path Made Clear*. Bluebird, 2019.

Zak, Paul J., 'The neuroscience of trust'. Harvard Business Review, January–February 2017, available at https://hbr.org/2017/01/the-neuroscience-of-trust.

Resources

Cool stuff we love dedicated to *LoveWork* principles:

Assessments

CliftonStrengths:
  Live your best life using your strengths and maximize your potential and work and everywhere else.
    https://www.gallup.com/cliftonstrengths/en/252137/home.aspx

Enneagram Test:
The Riso-Hudson Enneagram Type Indicator (RHETI® version 2.5). Understand your basic personality type to learn more about your intrinsic drivers.
    https://www.enneagraminstitute.com/rheti

Principles You:
  From Ray Dalio and Adam Grant – Gain the self awareness and other awareness that is critical to making good decisions and getting things done.
    https://principlesyou.com/

StandOut® strengths assessment:
The Gift of StandOut®. Learn about your greatest sources of strength and contribution.
    https://www.marcusbuckingham.com/gift-of-standout/

Books

Allcott, Graham, *How to be a Productivity Ninja*. Icon Books, 2016.
Worry Less, Achieve More, Love What you Do – tips and techniques.

Blakey, John, *The Trusted Executive*. Kogan Page, 2017.
Understanding the role of trust in leadership and organisations.

Cavoulacos, Alexandra, Minshew, Kathryn, *The New Rules of Work*. Crown Business, 2017.
The modern playbook to finding the perfect career path, landing the right job, and waking up excited for work every day, from founders of online network TheMuse.com.

Daisley, Bruce, *The Joy of Work*. Random House Business, 2020.
30 refreshingly simple tips on how to make your job more productive, more rewarding – and more enjoyable.

Edmondson, Amy, *The Fearless Organization*. Wiley, 2019.
Amy shows how to create the right climate for a continuous influx of new ideas, new challenges, and critical thought to achieve sustainable success at work.

Ellis, Sarah and Tupper, Helen, *The Squiggly Career*. Portfolio Penguin, 2020.
Packed with insights about the changing shape of work, exercises to fuel your growth and tips and inspiration from highly successful people, this book will help you be happier and ultimately more successful in your career.

Ferris, Tim, *The 4-Hour Work Week*. Vermilion, 2011.
Forget the old concept of retirement and the rest of the deferred-life plan - there is no need to wait and every reason not to, especially in unpredictable economic times.

Grant, Adam, *Give and Take*. Viking, 2013.
A ground-breaking look at why our interactions with others hold the key to success. Why givers – not takers or matchers – win big. Great perspectives on how positive relationships can lead to positive work and business success.

Kock, Richard, *The 80/20 Principle*. Nicholas Brealey Publishing, 2017.
Based on the counter-intuitive but widespread fact that 80% of results flow from 20% of causes, *The 80/20 Principle* shows how you can achieve much more with much less effort, time and resources, simply by concentrating on the all-important 20%.

Murden, Fiona, *Defining You*. Nicholas Brealey Publishing, 2018.
Work through a professional profiling assessment process in private to help you discover your strengths, understand what really drives you and learn which environments will help you to excel.

Pink, Dan, *Drive*. Penguin, Random House, 2009.
A seminal study (and highly readable book) looking at how to harness the power of intrinsic motivation rather than extrinsic remuneration in the workplace

Organizations

B Corporation

Certified B Corporations are businesses that meet the highest standards of verified social and environmental performance, public transparency, and legal accountability to balance profit and purpose. B Corps are accelerating a global culture shift to redefine success in business and build a more inclusive and sustainable economy.
   https://bcorporation.net/

Conscious capitalism

Conscious Capitalism, Inc. supports a global community of business leaders dedicated to elevating humanity through business. They provide mid-market executives with innovative and inspiring experiences designed to level-up their business operations and collectively demonstrate capitalism as a powerful force for good when practiced consciously.
   https://www.consciouscapitalism.org/

Culture Amp

A way of getting the employee engagement, performance and development tools and insights you need to build a category-defining culture.

https://www.cultureamp.com/

Dow Jones Sustainability Indices

The Dow Jones Sustainability Indices (DJSI) are a family of best-in-class benchmarks for investors who have recognized that sustainable business practices are critical to generating long-term shareholder value and who wish to reflect their sustainability convictions in their investment portfolios.

https://www.spglobal.com/esg/csa/indices/djsi-index-family

Great Place To Work

Has a mission to build a better world by helping organizations become a great place to work for all.

https://www.greatplacetowork.com

The House of Beautiful Business

Global platform, thinktank and community looking at humanity in business in age of machines and how to make business more beautiful.

https://houseofbeautifulbusiness.com/

Humu

Humu is an action management platform built for the enterprise that makes it easy for organizations to improve—every single week.

https://humu.com/

Tiny Pulse

Increase communication and transparency, improve and measure culture, and reduce company turnover.

https://www.tinypulse.com/

THE MUSE

The Muse is the go-to destination for the next gen workforce to research companies and careers.
  https://www.themuse.com/

WE ARE BEEP

Programmes and technology to unleash people-power in transformation programmes.
  https://wearebeep.com/

Podcasts

Aaker, Jennifer, Bagdonas, Naomi. Live Laugh Work – Understanding Humour At Work.
  Learn how to be better and happier at your job.
  https://eatsleepworkrepeat.com/live-laugh-work-understanding-humour-at-work/

Ferris, Tim, The Tim Ferriss Show: Jim Collins on The Value of Small Gestures, Unseen Sources of Power, and More.
  Discover 5 elements involved in guiding a company to lasting success and a blueprint for managing a thriving company.
  https://tim.blog/2020/11/30/jim-collins-returns/

Godin, Seth. Ask The Expert: Ideas with Seth Godin
  Learn about how to create idea rich cultures at work and how habits can help us share more ideas with the world.
  https://www.amazingif.com/listen/ask-the-expert-ideas-with-seth-godin/

Grant, Adam. WorkLife: Career Decline Isn't Inevitable
  Adam reminds us that we spend a quarter of our lives at work, therefore we should enjoy it! Learn the keys to a better work life.
  https://podcasts.apple.com/gb/podcast/career-decline-isnt-inevitable/id1346314086

TED

Brown, Brené, The Power of Vulnerability, 2010.

Brené studies human connection -- our ability to empathize, belong, love. In a poignant, funny talk, she shares a deep insight from her research, one that sent her on a personal quest to know herself as well as to understand humanity.

https://www.ted.com/talks/brene_brown_the_power_of_vulnerability

Waldinger, Robert. What makes a good life? Lessons from the longest study on happiness.

What keeps us happy and healthy as we go through life? If you think it's fame and money, you're not alone – but, according to psychiatrist Robert Waldinger, you're mistaken.

https://www.ted.com/talks/robert_waldinger_what_makes_a_good_life_lessons_from_the_longest_study_on_happiness

Pink, Daniel, The puzzle of motivation, 2010.

Career analyst Dan Pink examines the puzzle of motivation, starting with a fact that social scientists know but most managers don't: Traditional rewards aren't always as effective as we think.

https://www.ted.com/talks/dan_pink_the_puzzle_of_motivation

Sinek, Simon, How great leaders inspire action, 2009.

Simon made a discovery which profoundly changed his view on how he thought the world worked. He calls it the golden circle based on Why? How? What? It explains why some organizations and some leaders are able to inspire where others aren't.

https://www.ted.com/talks/simon_sinek_how_great_leaders_inspire_action

About the authors

© Nudge Photography

Ben Renshaw is one of today's foremost leadership thinkers. Speaker, coach and author, Ben's innovative work with leading organisations, senior executives and entrepreneurs has brought him international acclaim. Formerly a classical violinist, Ben now plays a different tune, getting the best out of people. He writes about how to lead and be successful in today's volatile world and is the author of ten popular books including Being, Purpose, LEAD and SuperCoaching. Ben's signature leadership development programmes include 'Leading with Purpose', 'Leading Change', and 'Leading Sustainable Growth'. As an executive coach and leadership consultant Ben has worked with clients like Allen & Overy, Aman Resorts, Barclays, Britvic, BT, Coca-Cola, Ghirardelli, Heathrow, Heinz, Henley Business School, Imperial College Business School, InterContinental Hotels Group, KPMG, London Underground, Mandarin Oriental, M&S, P&G, Rolls Royce, Sainsbury's, Shiseido, Sky, UBS, Unilever, Virgin Media and Warner Bros. https://benrenshaw.com

© Nudge Photography

Sophie Devonshire is the CEO of The Marketing Society, the global network of marketing leaders. As an experienced business leader and entrepreneur, her career includes brand management at Procter & Gamble and Coca-Cola, brand strategy for Interbrand and Group Account Director for Leo Burnett in the Middle East, as well as founding and selling an e-commerce business. Sophie mentors, coaches, and consults across the globe in a variety of organisations from start-ups to multinationals and is passionate about the positive role business should play in society. She is regularly invited by the media to comment on businesses and brands and is a popular keynote speaker on marketing, brands and leadership in a fast-paced world. Sophie is the author of *Superfast: Lead at Speed* which was shortlisted for the Business Book Awards and was the #1 bestseller in Change Management on Amazon.

Contact

To find out more about our speaking, coaching, team & leadership programmes or for media requests, please visit golovework.com.

Email: hello@golovework.com
LinkedIn: go-love-work
Instagram: @GoLoveWork
Twitter: @GoLoveWork

Acknowledgements

Sophie and Ben: A big part of doing what we love is working with brilliant people and being able to say thank you for the inspiration, energy, wisdom and support they provide. We want to thank the expert team at John Murray Press for their belief and support: Jonathan Shipley (commissioning editor); Jen Campbell (project editor); Lily Bowden (marketing manager) as well as Clare Weatherill for her support with our marketing and website and Ged Equi (cover design). Thank you to our photographer Noel Yeo (nudgephotography.com) for his expert eye and patience. Thank you to our extraordinary thought leaders for their insight and time who are named in the Contributors section. A special thank you to Amy Edmondson, Novartis Professor of Leadership and Management at the Harvard Business School and author of The Fearless Organization who generously wrote our foreword.

Sophie: Thank you to the fantastic team at The Marketing Society (marketingsociety.com) who play such an important role in helping me love my work, together with the Members and marketing leaders across the world who constantly inspire me with their stories, insights, creativity and brilliance in business.

Ben: Thank you to my current clients who have shaped my thinking for *LoveWork*: Allen & Overy; Aman Resorts; Britvic; Camlin; Cromwell; Edyn; European Bank for Reconstruction and Development; InComm Payments; Francis Crick Institute; Ghiarardelli Chocolate; Heathrow; The Henley Partnership; Inspired Villages; InterContinental Hotels Group; Kingfisher; Mandarin Oriental Hotels; Sainsbury's; Shangri-La Hotels & Resorts; Simplyhealth; The Standard; Transport for London; UBS; Warner Bros; Wyndham Destinations. Thank you to my mentors who have challenged me to learn and grow: Andreas Thrasyvolou, Chairman New World Hospitality; Graham Alexander, Founder The Alexander Partnership; Grant Fuzi, Co-CEO & Founder The Bridge Hub; Simon Woodroffe, Founder YO! Sushi. Thank you to my father, Peter Renshaw, for your generous support in reading the manuscript.